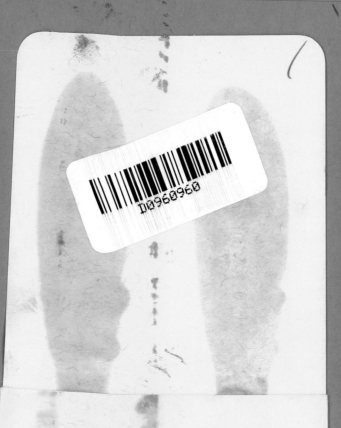

B+T 8.95

861

GIFFORD
ON COURAGE

Frank Gifford

with Charles Mangel

GIFFORD
ON COURAGE

M. EVANS AND COMPANY, INC. / New York, N.Y. 10017

The authors wish to thank the following publishers for permission to use material included:

Excerpts on pages 146, 147, 153, and 170 from *I Pass!* by Y.A. Tittle, Jr. as told to Don Smith. Copyright © 1964 by J. L. Pratt & Co., Inc. Used by permission of the publisher, Franklin Watts, Inc.

Excerpts from *The Open Man: A Championship Diary* by David DeBusschere, edited by Paul D. Zimmerman and Dick Schaap. Copyright © 1970 by David DeBusschere and Paul D. Zimmerman. Reprinted by permission of Random House, Inc.

Excerpts from *Fighting Back* by Rocky Bleier. Copyright © 1975 by Rocky Bleier. Reprinted with the permission of Stein & Day/Publishers.

M. Evans and Company titles are distributed in
the United States by the J. B. Lippincott Company,
East Washington Square, Philadelphia, Pa. 19105;
and in Canada by McClelland & Stewart Ltd.,
25 Hollinger Road, Toronto M4B, 3G2, Ontario

LIBRARY OF CONGRESS CATALOGING IN PUBLICATION DATA

Gifford, Frank, 1930-
    Gifford on courage.

    CONTENTS: Herb Score.—Rocky Bleier.—Charley
Boswell. [etc.]
    1. Athletes—United States—Biography.   I. Mangel,
Charles, joint author.   II. Title.
GV697.A1G47   796'.092'2 [B]   76-21862
ISBN 0-87131-223-9

Design by Joel Schick

Manufactured in the United States of America

9 8 7 6 5 4 3 2 1

Contents

Foreword

I like heroes. They have a marked impact on my life, and digging out the complete story of the following individuals' accomplishments has been one of the most enjoyable trips of my life.

It's been said that courage comes in many packages . . . the wrappings and ribbons often obliterating its real substance. In Yelberton Abraham Tittle, this is decidedly the case. True, the ol' baldheaded one had a great career, a career climaxed with recent enshrinement in the pro football Hall of Fame. But in following Y. A.'s journey with a pigskin from the rock-hard playing fields of little Marshall, Texas, to Kezar Stadium in San Francisco and Yankee Stadium in New York, you might be shocked to find that it almost didn't happen. No, Y.A. didn't have to overcome a damaging physical injury to achieve his goals in football. He did, however, have to dig deep within himself for the courage to overcome a painful self-doubt that came dangerously close to eliminating his most productive and, ultimately, his happiest years.

Then how about Don Klosterman? Courage in his story should be spelled with a capital "K." Don Klosterman, an All-American quarterback from Loyola University, a fun-loving, joke-spouting, budding star in the Canadian League, who skied like he played football—one way, all out. Skied, that is, until a terrifying crash in one bone-shattering instant brought Don face-to-face with a crisis few men have ever confronted. The first battle was the ultimate one. Given the last rites not once, but twice, Don battled back only to be told he'd never walk again. Again, the battle . . . and, again, the victory. The story—one of the most gripping I've ever known.

Dan Gable has a Gold Medal for his incredible performance in Munich on our U.S. wrestling team. Five other members of that team also came away with medals—the best record ever by a U.S. wrestling team. In my estimation all must share part of their treasured medals with Dan Gable, whose courageous example of dedication and self-sacrifice convinced them they *could* win.

Charlie Conerly of the New York Giants will perhaps never make the pro football Hall of Fame. Yet, if there was a way to measure his contributions over the years to a mediocre team, the Hall would not be big enough. Like Y. A. Tittle, Charlie, my old roommate, met head-on the fear of self-doubt in his early years and climaxed a glittering career by being voted the NFL's Player of the Year.

What has happened to the many players implicated in the basketball scandal of the 1951–1952 season? Many of them, tainted and shamed, have never been heard from again. Not so Floyd Layne, CCNY's junior guard, who was a starting member of the 1950–1951 squad, the only team ever to win both the NCAA tournament and the NIT. The glamour and glory of that year disappeared the following season as Layne was implicated in the point-shaving scandal, expelled from CCNY, and given a suspended jail sentence. The easy way would have been obscurity, but Layne took the tough way— dedicating his life to teaching the sport he loved to ghetto kids of the South Bronx. Eighteen years later, Layne came back to CCNY as the head basketball coach.

Charley Boswell is another name not so widely known.

Charley, who makes his home in Mississippi, is a laughing, good-natured, highly successful insurance man. He also travels far and wide, collecting a variety of hardware in the form of golf trophies. That's not unusual, of course—an insurance man who's a top golfer—but Charley *is* unusual. Charley Boswell is blind. His is a gripping story, much like that of Herb Score, who knew the fear that he might be blinded, and, surviving that, faced the agonizing fact that one of the most gifted talents ever to come into baseball had disappeared. Charley lost his sight in a heroic act during World War II . . . Herb Score lost his incredibly fast right arm on a baseball mound, almost before his career had begun. Both could have ambled through life, bitter and resentful. Neither has . . . offering proof, once again, that courage comes in a variety of packages.

Remember Willis Reed? New York basketball fans never will forget this tall, stoic, graceful athlete from the South. In a single basketball game—the final game of the 1969 NBA Championship series between the Knicks and the Los Angeles Lakers—Willis wrote the book on sheer physical courage. The Knicks would have lost that night without Reed. They won because the big man, defying all medical logic, limped onto the court, staggered through a pain-wracked two hours of battling Wilt Chamberlain, and lifted his teammates to an unbelievable victory.

And speaking of staggering—I've never seen a more dramatic scene in sports than Ken Venturi, reeling down the 18th fairway of Washington's Congressional Country Club. It was the final hole of the 1964 U.S. Open Championship. If he could stay on his feet on that blistering hot day, the stigma of his loss at the Masters in 1960 would be erased—the stigma that had had a devastating effect on one of the potentially finest golfers ever to swing a club. An inner strength and courage brought Ken home that day, just as that same strength and courage would bring him through the physically debilitating years ahead. His is a story for those who have ever had thoughts of giving up.

So, too, is the story of Rocky Bleier—the Pittsburgh Steelers' Rocky Bleier, who led the way for Franco Harris's record performances in Super Bowls IX and X. Rocky Bleier was never supposed to be a professional football player. As a steady, hardworking halfback at Notre Dame, Bleier may have impressed the alumni, but he never impressed the professional scouts. When he was drafted by the Steelers upon graduation, it was almost as an afterthought. "Not big but really slow" was one coach's laughing comment. But Rocky was big where it counted. His courage and determination were to surface in Vietnam long before he ever saw a Steeler practice field. Wounded by shrapnel and rifle fire, Rocky made an unusual pact with God that grim day in 1969: he asked for his life and offered in return the willingness to do the best he could with it. The prayer granted, Rocky returned from Vietnam a shadow of his former self and with a damaged leg and foot that made walking difficult and running unthinkable. No one gave Rocky a thought when he joined the Steelers in 1970—much less the new head coach, Chuck Noll, whose job it was to build a team, not cater to handicap cases. Rocky's ascendance to stardom has been well documented. Not so well documented were the strength and courage he called upon to make it happen.

These, then, are the stories that follow. Each and every one of us could use some of the courage displayed by these men.

Herb
Score

It was Bob Feller all over again. A kid who could move from the dirt ballfield and splintered stands behind the high school gym right into the major leagues and take on Williams and Mantle and the rest on even terms. He had a fast ball that Yogi Berra called "unfair," a curve that broke almost at a right angle, and if he could only get his control into shape, why he was sure to win 20 games his first year and, lord, maybe into infinity.

He set people dreaming. Even hard-nosed pros, who watched pretenders come up and go down every year, saw visions: Hal Newhouser, Prince Hal, the strongman of the Detroit pitching staff finishing his career with Cleveland, said, "I wish I had his future rather than my past." Tris Speaker, the old centerfielder against whom all centerfielders are measured, said, "He'll be the greatest." Flat out. No qualification. Men who played with Feller said the kid's fast ball was faster than Feller's and if Feller disagreed he kept it to himself.

His first trip—age 18—to meet the Cleveland brass might have been the wish of a Little Leaguer. "Just warm up, son, and we'll see what you have." The first few pitches crack into the catcher's mitt and a coach roars out of the dugout screaming, "I told you to take it easy; don't bear down until you're warm." And the apologetic response: "I'm not bearing down, sir." The catcher surreptitiously slips a sponge rubber pad into his glove.

We revel in new heroes, a fresh name to take its place beside Grove, Alexander, Johnson, Spahn in the pantheon of our memories. Young, skinny Herb Score seemed destined. Three fantastic years in succession, one in the highest rung of the minors, two in the majors. He wins 36 and loses 19 those two years with Cleveland. He strikes out 245 the first year and 263 the second. Both records. (Feller didn't strike out 240 until his third year; Grove, whom many call the best lefthander ever, until his sixth.) He wins Rookie of the Year in the minors and repeats the next year with Cleveland.

Then he's through. He doesn't have another winning season. In the baseball vernacular, he loses his arm.

Herb Score. Mention his name even to a marginal baseball fan and you'll hear, "Oh, yeah, he was the guy who was hit in the eye by McDougald's line drive. Shame. Great promise. Knocked him right out of baseball."

Did it? How *does* an arm go bad? When a spur begins to grow? When strain distorts a tendon? When the chill of a spring night game subtly alters musculature? When a baseball traveling 130 miles an hour smashes into an eye? So much the magic of medicine can't tell us; along with the diseases that ravage man, why does a pitcher suddenly lose his arm?

Herbert Score, 41 and totally gray, sportscaster for the Indians, is doing some missionary work before a room jammed with members of the Napoleon, Ohio, Kiwanis Club (they even permitted a few eager wives in this night; but *after* dinner). Score speaks well, with a fine self-directed wit.

"During my first season with Cleveland, we made an early visit to New York where I was born. I was hoping to pitch against the Yankees. I figured I'd walk onto that field and every kid I'd gone to school with would be there and I'd show them what I'd become. But Al Lopez was a bright manager. He wasn't going to use me. It would be Early Wynn Friday night, Mike Garcia Saturday and Bob Lemon Sunday. Saturday afternoon, Lemon is running in the outfield and pulls a muscle in his leg. After the game Saturday, Lopez tells me, 'We don't know if Lemon's leg will be all right tomorrow. If he can't pitch, you're going to start against the Yankees. Get to bed early tonight.'

"Next morning it's Sunday and I decide to go to St. Patrick's Cathedral. I'm in there kneeling, praying. And as I'm meditating and praying, I said, 'Lord, Bob Lemon hurt his leg yesterday. They don't know how serious it is and he's been awfully nice to me, taken me to dinner. He's a great pitcher, won 20 games six or seven times and he's just an outstanding person. But if you could see your way clear he couldn't walk today, I'd appreciate it.'

"I get to the ballpark and they're still not sure if Lemon's going to be able to play, so they tell us both to warm up. If Lemon's leg doesn't hurt, he'll pitch. About 10 minutes go by and they decide he's okay and tell me to sit down. It's about time for the game to start and rather than run across the field to the bullpen, I decide to walk underneath the stadium concourse.

"I start out and I'm passing the concessions. You know, nothing smells as good as hot dogs at a ballpark. Absolutely nothing. I'm walking and I'm smelling. If I only had some money, I'd buy some hot dogs. In those days, I was always hungry. I strike up a conversation with a couple of fellows. Pretty soon I have two hot dogs. I keep walking and I hear the game start. At the head of the ramp going down to the bullpen, there's another concession stand. I thought, the hot dogs were good. A little ice cream to wash it down wouldn't be bad. Sure enough, another conversation; I end up with a box of ice cream.

"Sit down on the bench and by now the Yankees are at

bat. I open my shirt, take off my cap, close my eyes and I'm ready to take a little sun. All of a sudden, I feel a tug at my sleeve and I open my eyes and there's Mel Harder, our pitching coach. He's pointing toward the mound. I see Lopez standing there waving his left hand. Harder says, 'I think he wants you.' And I say, 'That's what I'm afraid of.'

"I climb over the railing and start across the outfield toward the mound. Yankee Stadium, 60,000 people, something I've dreamed of since I was a kid and here I am gurgling with every step.

"Finally get to the mound, Lopez tells me Lemon's leg is hurting, the umpires realize this and I can take all the time I need to warm up. I figured it might take three days. But we get under way and it gets into the fifth or sixth inning and somehow the Yankees load the bases and there are no outs. I look up and here's Mickey Mantle at the plate. We all know there's a lot of criticism of baseball for being a long game, being too slow, and usually they blame the pitcher and they say how come he holds the ball so long. As long as I'm holding it, he can't hit it.

"I know I have to do something and then I hear someone call time out. Al Rosen's playing third base, sort of the unofficial team captain. He's called time and he's going to walk over and I know I'm going to get this wonderful piece of advice.

"Rosen calls the shortstop and they have a little meeting. Now Rosen comes to the mound. He and the shortstop have worked it all out. 'Hey kid,' he says, 'you're really in trouble.'

"The mind is a wonderful thing and frequently we're able to forget unhappy events. I don't remember the details from that point, except learning why Mantle is paid all that salary, but I'm young and I'll have lots of chances at the Yankees and we continue to Boston.

"I had heard a lot about Ted Williams and I'm looking

forward to pitching against him. So the first time we play the Red Sox, I'm geared up to face Williams. But he's not in the line-up. Has the flu. Two weeks later, we have another series with Boston. And again, I'm ready for Williams. Again, he's not in the line-up. A suspicion grows. Possibly Williams doesn't want to face Score. It's understandable. He's getting on—34, 35 years old—and his reflexes are shot and he possibly couldn't get around on a fast ball any more. I'd been having a good spring. Won a couple of games. I could understand his reluctance.

"It gets to be June and the Red Sox are in Cleveland. Finally, Williams is going to meet Score. I know this because they have it in the newspaper and they're never wrong. I could hardly wait to warm up. It's the first inning and here comes Williams, batting third. I'm not the kind of pitcher, incidentally, who looks back to see where his fielders are playing each batter. I didn't know where I was going to throw it, so I sure didn't know where they were going to hit it.

"But I notice suddenly that the team is shifting way over to the right, the Boudreau shift. The shortstop is on the right side of second base, the second baseman almost in right field, Rosen all alone on the left side of the infield. I was thinking, if I say anything to them, they'll think I'm a fresh rookie and I shouldn't talk, all those veteran ballplayers. There's no way Williams can pull me, not *my* fast ball, but I figure they'll find out for themselves. Count gets to be three balls and a strike and Williams hits a little fly ball into left centerfield.

"The Cleveland stadium sits out there on the lake and very unusual wind currents blow off the water. Somehow this ball gets up into one of those unusual currents and that lazy fly ball hits the fence 385 feet away. Williams has a double. I'm undaunted. He didn't *pull* the ball. When he comes up next time, I'll reach back, give it a little extra push and zip right on by him. He comes up two innings later, I reach back for a little extra, he hits it into the upper deck in right field. In his first 16 times at bat, Williams hits four home runs, a double, and a single off me.

"So, next trip to Boston, Williams is in the line-up again. He's obviously regained his confidence as far as Score is concerned. Now I've rarely been able to get ahead of Williams. It's always two balls and no strikes, three balls and maybe one strike. I have two pitches, a fast ball and a curve, and the curve I usually don't get over. So if you want to guess what's coming, you have a pretty good percentage. I'd have Williams 3–0 and he'd say to himself, he's going to throw me a fast ball and I'm going to hit it 100 miles. And I'd say to myself, I'm going to throw him a fast ball and he's going to hit it 100 miles.

"But, now, I do get ahead of him. I get two strikes, no balls. I've got him. I've pitched a whole year and I know how to do this. I'm going to bounce the curve in front of home plate. Then I'm going to stomp around on the mound and kick some dirt and fume and Williams is going to say, ahah, he still can't get that curve over. Then I'm going to throw a fast ball right up under his chin. He's going to jump back and he's going to say, ahah, now he'll have to come in with a fast ball and then I'm going to throw the curve over the outside corner; he'll be so surprised he won't even swing, strike three. All figured out.

"I bounce the curve in front of the plate, stomp around, put on a pretty good show. Now I'm ready. Someone once told me it takes two-fifths of a second from the time a pitcher releases until the batter swings. You'd be amazed what goes through your mind in two-fifths of a second. I throw the ball. I see him start to swing. I notice he has a lovely swing. I see the ball over my head, and I think, boy, he sure didn't pull my pitch. I look back and all I can see is the centerfielder's number. I'm thinking, it carried pretty good, Larry Doby's going to have to hurry to catch it. Then I realize he's not going to catch it. He's going to play it off the wall in center-field. Then I realize it's not going to hit the wall."

His audience warm, Score talked about prospects for the current Indians and then asked for questions. Two routine queries, and a hand goes up hesitantly: "Herb, what happened with McDougald?" Nineteen years later and they still ask. A pitcher with extraordinary skills loses them and people still wonder.

Six no-hitters and three perfect games in three years of high school ball, a total of eight hits allowed his entire junior year, brought scouts from 14 of the then-16 major league teams to his family's home. Ten offered bonuses up to $80,000 if he would sign with them; four said simply, "Tell us your best offer and we'll top it."

Herb and his mother had very little money but passed up the dollar hunt and chose a friend instead. Cy Slapnicka, the man who had signed Feller as a 17-year-old in Iowa, wintered in Score's hometown of Lake Worth, Florida. Told by a city cop one day about a freshman at Lake Worth High, Slapnicka went to watch—and kept his seat behind home plate for three seasons. Major league rules prevented him from talking contract until the youngster turned 19; but he could talk about other things, couldn't he? He could take Herb, his mother and two sisters out to dinner now and then. And, if the talk got around to baseball, he might mention a few of the nice things about the people he worked for. There's no law against that, is there?

So Slap and the family became genuinely great friends. And by the start of Herb's junior year, when the other scouts began to show in packs, it really was too late. (Even though Herb coincidentally had been dating the pretty daughter of one of them.) Slap offered $60,000. Herb took it, bought his mother a house and himself a record player.

Baseball was more than a game to Score, however talented

he was; it was—well, it was communication. He was—still is —shy and modest. But intense, too, if that doesn't seem contradictory. "The reason I played so hard at baseball," he says, "was because that was the one thing *I could do,* the only thing that would lift me out of the crowd. We had no money. People knew my father drank a lot and someone would come by and say your father's down there somewhere drunk. My parents separated. We moved to Florida and sports was the only way I could 'say' something."

Some intangible within Score forced him to make his "statement" clear and sharp. "Players, great players, come to the majors all the time with extraordinary talent," says Rocky Colavito, Score's friend, teammate, and later, a coach, "but often they try to get by with just their God-given skills. I never saw any pitcher come up with the natural equipment Herb had, but that wasn't enough for him. He made perfect seem like second-rate. He had a burning desire to excel. In warm-ups he didn't jog, he ran. In playing catch along the sidelines, he didn't lob. He threw. Even after he won a game, he talked to me for hours about how *he* might have played better. He wouldn't accept an average performance."

No one could ever suggest that Score was not giving his best. In Indianapolis, manager Kerby Farrell walked out to the mound to remove Score after he had walked three successive batters. "Herb," he said, "you're not trying to relax." Score didn't hear the last two words and snapped, "Get away from me before I push your nose through your face." Score left the game and put the runway to the locker room into temporary eclipse by breaking every light bulb en route. Then he tore the locker room apart. Suddenly, Herb realized what he had done. From that point he kept his furies to himself. "If I don't pitch well, why should I take it out on other people?" he told me. "Why should people have to walk carefully around me?" No one, in the ballpark or at home, ever saw him angry again. When he was displeased with the way he pitched, he would wait until he got into his car after the game, roll up the windows and scream at the top of his voice.

In demand from his first year in Cleveland as a speaker at sports affairs, Score was politic and always said what the audience wanted to hear. But there was one exception. At a high school dinner, the baseball coach preceded Score and said that while the team had not done too well, "We all had fun." Score, always slow to criticize, had to disagree. "I don't understand how you could have fun while you were losing. I'll tell you honestly, it kills me."

Every batter was Herb's personal antagonist. "Every hit against me was a slap in my face," he says. "I hated that batter." Score can't remember those he got out, but he will give you—30 years later—clinical details of everyone who hit him going back to high school. He didn't walk too many in those days because high school kids scare. They see a wild fastballer, take three strikes and sit down, relieved they're still whole.

At that, perhaps they weren't too different from major leaguers. Frank Frisch, manager and second baseman of the Cardinals, watched a fast, wild Feller warm up before pitching against the Cards in an exhibition game in 1936. After one of Feller's errant pitches splintered a section of the backstop, Frisch called rookie Lynn King.

"Young man," he asked, "have you ever played second base?"

"No sir," King replied.

"Well, you're playing there today."

Feller struck out eight men in the first three innings of that game. One of them was shortstop Leo Durocher. Durocher looked at the first two strikes and, as legend has it, turned and walked away.

"Wait a minute," the umpire said. "You have another strike coming."

"Thanks," said Durocher. "I don't want it."

Score could have come directly to the Indians when he signed his contract in June 1952, but there were Wynn, Lemon and Garcia, each winning 20 games a year or more, and Feller, fading but good for 10 or 15 wins a season. Lopez wanted Score to pitch regularly and get over his wildness. In the closing months of the '52 season, Score went to Indianapolis, the Indians' top farm club, and walked 62 in 62 innings. He was demoted to Reading. There the next year, he walked 126 in 98 innings (and during warmup one day badly dented a new car waiting alongside the first baseline to be given away).

The Indians brought Score back to Indianapolis for spring training in 1954 and turned the matter over to Ted Wilks, the old Cardinal reliever who was then the Indianapolis pitching coach. Wilks' style was unusual. He swore a lot. From the dugout in full earshot of two city blocks: "Keep your damn head level. Watch the goddamn plate. Look where you're throwing if you want the ball to get there."

A pitcher's motion is a many-faceted and fragile thing. Every part of the motion—kick, step, release, follow-through —must be synchronized if the ball is to get where the pitcher wants it, to a piece of a strike zone 17 inches wide. Before Wilks, Herb just leaned back as far as he could behind a high leg kick to get as much "body" into each throw as possible. But the kick pulled his head back so he lost sight of catcher, plate and batter. His head bobbed as he came forward. After Score released the ball, his hard delivery carried him so far forward that his left elbow slammed into his right knee. In self-defense, he had long before strapped a rubber pad to his knee.

Wilks lowered Score's leg kick considerably. He taught Score to pivot, to get his power by swiveling his hips rather than by tilting backward as much as he had. And to keep his eyes on the target until he released the ball. The follow-through wasn't changed much, however; Score frequently finished a pitch with his back turned to the plate. Score often had been hit by batted balls he never saw.

Herb remained with Wilks in 1954 and pitched Indianapolis to a pennant. He reduced his walks to 140 in 252 innings, acceptable by any measurement, struck out 330, won 22 games and lost only 5. He was hit hard in only one game all season, a 6–5 loss to Louisville. His other four losses: 2–1 twice, 1–0, 4–3. He was elected Most Valuable Player in the league as well as Rookie of the Year. *The Sporting News,* the sports bible, chose him the number-one player in the minor leagues.

Herb was extremely popular, too. He became an instant kid brother to many athletes whose careers had ended and were hanging on perhaps for another year or two. During Herb's first visit to Indianapolis, a former major league pitcher named Johnny Hutchings was a coach. Herb, extremely thin, always had trouble with his uniforms, especially the pants.

Because of his fierce windup, his socks and the bottom of each pant leg would fall down continually. Herb would spend much of each ball game pulling up his trousers and socks. One afternoon, Hutchings called time out, picked up a roll of tape, and walked out to the mound. A huge man, weighing well over 300 pounds, Hutchings bent over laboriously, pulled up one of Herb's pant legs, then pulled up the sock, taped the sock to the pant leg just above the calf, adjusted the pant leg, did the same with the other leg, pulled the trouser leg and sock up, taped it, adjusted it. All in slow motion. When he finished, he stepped back a pace or two to survey his work, then walked up to Herb, took off Herb's cap and kissed him on the cheek. (When Hutchings died 10 years later, his will asked that Herb be a pallbearer.)

Gossip in spring training is almost as much a part of that annual ritual as baseball itself. Two hundred and seventy-two minor leaguers were in camps in 1955—Elston Howard, Most Valuable Player in the International League the year before, and Ken Boyer among them—trying to win a spot in the majors. But it seemed most of the sportswriters were looking at the quiet lefthander from Indianapolis who was not yet old enough to vote.

In the hierarchy of baseball players, the fastballer stands first—higher than the Ruths, Aarons and Gehrigs. Brains can create a crafty pitcher, even a junk ball hurler who wins by virtue of experience and guile and, maybe, an occasional spitter. But a fireballer is nature's gift. And baseball men stand in awe. Dazzy Vance, an excellent speedballer in his own right, was warming up one day near the end of his career to pitch an exhibition against Feller, just 17. A photographer came up to Vance and asked if he would mind posing with the young kid. "Ask him," said Vance, "if he would mind posing with me." Hierarchies within hierarchies. Herb Score fit. He, with the classic overhand fireball delivered almost javelin-like with the full stretch of his six-foot-two body.

A natural pitching motion or a batter's natural swing can exceed for pure beauty most things created by man. John McGraw ordered 16-year-old Mel Ott not to take any hitting advice even though Ott swung with his forward foot up in the air. Lopez told Score he'd fine him if he ever saw Herb comparing pitching styles with the other men on the team. When Herb experimented one day with a change-up ball, a new pitch, Lopez threatened to send him back to Indianapolis.

At the Indians' camp in Tucson that spring in 1955, Score pitched as if he feared he would be cut. His reputation as a perfectionist had preceded him. Coaches watched to see that he didn't drive himself too hard. Score admitted to one writer that he "didn't know how to throw easy. Every batter is tough for me. I even bear down on the pitcher."

Herb had one goal—formed back in Rosedale, N.Y. when he was in eighth grade—and he didn't want to lose it now. He didn't have to worry. Cleveland couldn't keep him in the minors any longer. The club had won 111 games and the pennant in 1954 with Wynn, Lemon and Garcia winning 55 games among them and Feller contributing 13. Could Score crack that starting rotation? He could and Lemon soon was moved to coin a couplet of sorts: "There's no big four any more/Score's got to stay in the store."

The lefthander became the Indians' most effective pitcher that season. He struck out 245 batters in 227 innings—an average 9.70 for nine innings—breaking a 44-year-old record for rookies set by Grover Cleveland Alexander. No previous pitcher, not even Feller, had ever been able to strike out batters at that pace for a full season. Feller's best was 7.3, Walter Johnson's, 6.9. Score allowed only 2.85 earned runs per game, won 16 games and lost 10. Once again, he was voted Rookie of the Year. He pitched a one-hitter, a two-hitter, three three-hitters and struck out 16 batters in one game, only two less than the record of the time, 18, held by Feller. During one game in 1955, Detroit somehow successfully intercepted all of Herb's pitching signals, yet still lost, 3–1.

The following year was even better. Score won 20 and lost 9. He struck out 263—setting an unofficial freshman-sophomore record of 547—and brought his walks down to an average five per nine-inning game. He battled New York's Whitey Ford to the final days of the season for the earned-run title. Ford won with 2.47, .06 better than Score's. The Indian pitching staff slumped in 1956. Garcia was 11–12 and Feller was 0–4. "During the last half of the season," someone cracked, "Cleveland's big three were Score, Don Mossi and Ray Narleski." Mossi and Narleski were the Indians' relief pitchers. Even though the Indians lost the pennant to the

Yankees by nine games, attention focused on Score during the last half of the season as he won 10 games and lost only one. Few pros had ever seen anyone who could pitch almost as hard and effectively at the end of a game as at the beginning.

Wilks, at Indianapolis, continued to monitor Score, in person when he could, other times on television. When the Indians came to Indianapolis for periodic exhibition games, Wilks would always meet Score at the airport, bellowing for all to hear, "You're not keeping your goddamn eyes on the batter."

At spring training in 1957, Mickey Mantle—who was to bat .365 that season—called Score the toughest pitcher he had ever hit against; the Boston Red Sox offered Cleveland $1 million cash for Score, the largest bid ever made for a ballplayer (the worth of the entire Cleveland franchise was estimated at $3 million); and *The Sporting News* asked, "Will Score become the greatest lefthander in the history of baseball?"

Four weeks later, Score's career effectively ended. It was his fourth start of the season, May 7, and he was in the first inning against the Yankees. He retired Hank Bauer and then came Gil McDougald, Yankee shortstop. With the count 2 and 2, McDougald had to swing at the fast ball belt high on the outside. He lined it back at the pitcher's mound. Score, as usual, had turned his eyes away in his follow-through. He looked up in time to see a flash of white before the ball hit him squarely in the right eye.

He crumbled, but never lost consciousness. He had remarkable presence of mind. He poked around in his mouth to see if he had swallowed his bridgework. Then he felt his ears to determine if he was bleeding from them. He knew he was bleeding badly; he could taste the blood in his mouth and from his nose. Colavito raced in from right field and then stood there, helpless. He finally put his glove under Score's head so Herb's face wouldn't have to be on the dirt.

The public address system announcer asked if there were any doctors in the stands; within minutes, six were at the pitcher's mound. Score was carried into the clubhouse and placed on the trainer's table. Pain, the real pain, hadn't started yet. By this time, the team's doctor, driving nearby, had heard of the accident on the radio and reached the ballpark. He got there in time to hear Herb crack, "Now I know how Fullmer felt last week." (Ray Robinson only days earlier had punched Gene Fullmer silly in a middleweight title bout.) At the end of the inning, Colavito raced to the clubhouse to find out how Score was doing and was greeted by mock anger: "What are you doing here? Get back to work." An ambulance brought Score to a hospital where an ophthalmologist was waiting.

Herb asked only one question, "Am I blind?" The physician, Dr. Charles I. Thomas, said, "I don't know. I can't tell the condition of your eye because it's swollen and hemorrhaging so badly." Drugs were administered to help stop the bleeding. Herb asked for a radio so he could listen to the rest of the game. (Cleveland won.)

Dr. Thomas made Herb lie still. He didn't want any pupil movement. He bandaged the left eye so Score wouldn't move that pupil which of course would cause the pupil in the right eye to move as well. Then the pain began, from the pressure in the right eye and from the fracture in his nose and a displaced right cheekbone.

Herb lay still for eight days. By then, the swelling around the eye had receded sufficiently so Dr. Thomas was able to have a clear field. The retina had been torn, but not completely. The physician hoped that surgery to repair the rip would not be necessary. Score would not be blind in that eye but might have a blind spot.

Three weeks later, he was discharged. His vision from the damaged eye was blurred for almost a year. No one knew if he would pitch again. Herb had been placed on large doses of cortisone and it took five months to wean him from that drug. He was finished with baseball for the balance of the season.

No one suggested to Score that he might not be able to come back from the injury, but there was concern. Herb had little depth perception; he couldn't tell if a ball thrown to him was three or 30 feet away. Exercises during the winter returned his depth perception to normal. Score asked Colavito to report early to spring training with him so he could pitch to Rocky with the usual waist-high batting-practice shield removed. Colavito was hesitant, but Herb, in his customary straight-out manner, said, "Rocky, I've got to know if I'm gun shy and now is as good a time as any." Colavito sprayed line drives and grounders throughout the infield and pitching area; Score didn't let up.

Herb lost his first game of the season but seemed to dispel all doubts in his second start, against the Chicago White Sox. He gave up two hits, struck out 14 and won, 3–0. "That convinced me," he said, "that I have everything I had before the accident."

He still hadn't regained his old pitching rhythm, but he wasn't worried. Spring that year was cold and rainy, not ideal conditions for a pitcher, especially one who had laid off for a year. Rain washed out what would have been Score's next two starts. Nine days later, he opened against the Senators on a damp, cold night. He was winning in the fourth inning when he attempted a curve and felt a strain in his forearm just below the elbow. In the seventh inning, a fast ball failed to reach the batter. Actually bounced in front of the plate. Incredulously, Herb tried again; same result. Now his arm began to hurt. He called manager Bobby Bragan to the mound and told him what happened. Score left the game. Next morning, his arm was swollen so badly he could hardly get it through the sleeve of his coat.

He was examined by the Washington team's physician who told him to rest the arm for a few days. Five days later, Herb tried to throw again. The pain was unbearable. Score consulted the Indians' doctor. He advised him not to pitch for 10 days. After 10 days, the arm continued to hurt, but Score thought he could work the pain out by throwing.

Finally, Herb went to Johns Hopkins, one of the outstanding hospitals in the country. There, he was told that he had torn a tendon back in April against Washington. Again, Herb was told to rest the arm, this time for 30 days. He obeyed, then began to throw again, in warmups, in batting practice, trying to get his arm back into condition. He threw hard a couple of times and felt no pain. Bragan asked him if he thought he could finish the last three innings of a game in Washington. Score got nine consecutive batters out, six by strike-outs. On the last pitch of the game, Score felt a sharp stabbing pain in his arm again, this time accompanied by a popping sound in his elbow.

Again the arm blew up. Score rested several weeks, then began to throw. He could still break off his curve as effectively as ever but his arm hurt every time he attempted a fast ball. Anxious about the amount of time he had missed, he began to press. He modified his throwing motion slightly to end the pain from the fast ball and told Bragan he was ready to go.

Several days later, he was called in from the bullpen in the fourth inning against the Yankees. (Ironically, the first batter was McDougald, the first time they had faced each other since the accident.) Herb had nothing on the ball except a curve and a slow change of pace—the same pitch Lopez had banned angrily two years earlier. Score struck out McDougald and finished the game without giving up any runs. But he knew he couldn't throw well.

The agony lasted the remainder of that season—he finished

with 2 wins and 3 losses. "I had spent practically two full seasons without pitching," Herb said. "All that time, I was developing bad habits. When I tried to work, I favored my elbow. If I threw low in a certain way, I wouldn't strain my arm, but I lost my fluid motion and my rhythm and I never recovered it." At midyear in 1959, Score had won nine games and lost four, mainly by careful use of his curve and the change-up. He no longer had the looseness he had before. He was throwing as hard, but the ball was nowhere near as fast as it had been.

Yet, 9–4 at the All-Star midyear break; he wasn't doing too badly. Joe Gordon, the new manager, suggested cutting down Herb's full motion drastically. Herb put unfamiliar stresses on his arm. He became a sore-arm pitcher. As his confidence began to ebb, so did his remaining effectiveness. He didn't win another game that season and lost seven more.

Gordon and general manager Frank Lane gave up on Score. Indian management would not let Herb be traded to anyone but Lopez, his first-year manager who was then handling the White Sox. Lopez had been watching his former pitcher closely and had seen what he believed were flashes of the 1955 Score. Shortly before the 1960 season began, Score, age 27, went to the Sox.

"Of course, there was an element of selfishness to it," Lopez says. "I hoped to profit by having Herb make good with the White Sox. But I also had another motive. In all my years in baseball, I never met a finer man. I felt I might be able to help him."

Lopez, some said, brought the guesswork of handling a pitcher to an art form. Perhaps it was his training as a catcher. He had the uncanny ability, for example, to pull a pitcher out of a game before maximum damage was done. He seemed to *know* before a pitcher stayed a bit too long, before a fast ball failed to jump, before a curve started to roll, even before a man's spirit failed. He never asked a pitcher. And for some reason understood by none, he was usually right.

But Lopez had no magic for Herb. The ordeal was not to end. Score started 22 games that year, finished only five. In six of those early games, he made it past the fourth inning only once. He twice put 12 runners on base in less than four innings. "I was throwing the ball well and the pain was gone. But I just couldn't hit a groove, get the ball over. When I did get it over, there wasn't that much on it." There were brief moments, even games, when "all of a sudden, it looked like it was coming back. Then—nothing." He began "aiming" the ball, placing too much emphasis on his arm in an attempt to get the ball where it should go; in the process, whatever "stuff" he had on the ball would disappear.

The next season was worse; Herb started five games, finished one. About midseason, Score opened a night game in Baltimore, pitched to five batters and allowed four runs before Lopez sent in another pitcher.

Neither Lopez nor Score had an easy answer. And, of course, there was none. Herb felt well, the best in years, he told Chicago writers. Why was he pitching so "lousy," as he put it?

Lopez suggested Herb go down to San Diego, then a minor league team, for several weeks. There he could work regularly, pitch every four days in rotation, something not possible with Chicago. Herb, after talking it over with Nancy, a classmate from Lake Worth High whom he had married in 1957, agreed.

So Score went to San Diego. "In my own mind, I knew that I would never be what I once was," he said afterward. "But I was hoping that I could still pitch reasonably well, still win." His delivery became a parody of what it had been. He kept getting extreme periods of wildness, worse than when he had been a rookie. His arm would come to a kind of halt at the end of the windup and he seemed to be pushing the ball.

The old natural motion when he just reared back and threw now was replaced with constant planning. He explained it to writer Jack Olsen: "If I throw the ball and I haven't followed through or I land wrong, this would tell me that I'm not throwing right and I would say to myself, 'Let me pivot a little slower, let me bring my arm up higher,' and these are things you don't normally have to think about. You should get the sign from the catcher; then the only thing you should think about is I'm gonna throw this fast ball low and across the inside and concentrate only on that. But I would wind up and tell myself, 'Now make sure you pivot right, don't lean back too far, hold your head level,' and you can't do all that. And then I get behind a batter, maybe two balls and no strikes, and I begin to aim. I'd be better off if I just slung the ball and it wound up in the grandstand."

One holiday in San Diego, Score started the first game of a doubleheader against Seattle. He faced 11 batters in two innings, gave up two home runs, a double, two singles and walked three. He was brought in to relieve in the fourth inning of the second game. Seattle reached him for two singles, two doubles, two triples and six runs. In four innings, the pitcher who was to surpass Grove had given up 13 runs. In 133⅔ innings at San Diego, he walked 136, made 15 wild pitches, allowed 103 hits.

He went to the minors twice more after San Diego. In 1962 and again in 1963, he attempted a comeback with Indianapolis where he had started. He would not quit until he was sure he had given himself the time he needed. "I didn't want to think 15 years later that I could have pitched if I had tried a little longer. I went out and proved I couldn't pitch." *Then* it was time to stop.

"I'm grateful to have played in the major leagues and to

have had some degree of success," he told reporters then. "I'm retiring sooner than I wanted to. That's nothing to be sad about."

As a measure of the respect men throughout baseball had for him, he was immediately asked to come back to Cleveland to broadcast its games. And that seemed fine to him. Because he loved baseball and now could stay with it.

Many skilled athletes have legends created about them: Williams, full of self-generated demons but, often, as gentle as a child; Cobb, noisy, hostile and cruel; Koufax, shy and private but extraordinarily principled. Score, too, created a legend quite apart from his ballplaying: a good man with the potential for athletic greatness who didn't complain when the vision died young. Lopez, his first—and last—major league manager may have said it best: "Herb, if my son was to be a baseball player, you're the one I'd want him to model himself after."

Courage is an ill-defined term. Certainly, it is not the exclusive property of athletes who come back from problems to their former renown. It belongs, too, to those like Score who labor with little success for six years in the hope they may find some part of their former brillance. Score found none and who is to blame it on the eye injury or the torn tendon? Who even cares? He could have quit many times and none would have raised a voice against him. I know many athletes, in a variety of sports, who have quit for less —and demanded public sympathy as well.

What must it be like to realize that an eighth-grade dream —a reality well into manhood—is perishing? Within the context of sports, Herb's story is one of the saddest I know. Talent so great should wither gracefully so the rest of us can prepare for the end of something bestowed on few. One talks now to Herb and Nancy and expects to find—what? Disappointment—certainly. Bitterness—possibly. After all he was "sure" to make the Hall of Fame. He began pitching when salaries were just beginning to rival those of movie starlets. Not small losses. Yet he laughs when I suggest fate played a poor trick on him and turns the topic to something else.

Long after Herb went into decline, he was pitching the second game of a doubleheader against the Red Sox. It was late in the season, the temperature was about 94° and neither team was going anywhere in the pennant race. Score had absolutely nothing on the ball. Pitching just by instinct, he kept the Sox scoreless. His team managed a run to go ahead, 1–0, entering the ninth inning. Score got the first two batters out.

Ted Williams no longer played the second game of doubleheaders, but now he came in to pinch-hit. Score was perspiring, sick about the season he was having and struggling with every pitch. He got two strikes on Williams. Always an overhand pitcher, Score experimented with a side arm curve and, because of his fatigue or maybe his sweaty fingers slipped, the ball took a couple of unexpected dips. Williams stared at it—the pitch was a long time getting to the plate —and he finally swung as if he had an axe in his hand, almost straight down, and he missed.

Score didn't know it, but that was the last shut-out he would pitch in the majors. His arm was dead and hurting and he knew it was a matter of time before he would have to stop playing. But on that hot Sunday in Boston with absolutely nothing at stake he had to win.

Pete Reiser, the old Dodger outfielder, would understand that. Reiser crashed into so many outfield walls trying to catch long drives that he shortened his career considerably. One July afternoon in 1942, Brooklyn was leading the league by 13½ games and the Cardinals were in town. It was the second game of a doubleheader, there was no score and it was in extra innings. Enos Slaughter belted a ball deep to centerfield. Racing for it, Reiser thought, "If I don't get it, it's a triple and there could go the game."

He slammed into the wall at full speed, dropped the ball and knocked himself out. In the hospital, he learned he had a fractured skull, "Was I being foolhardy in going after that ball the way I did?" Reiser asked years later.* "After all, we had a 13½ game lead. . . . You can slow up in those circumstances, can't you? No, you can't. You slow up a half step and it's the beginning of your last ball game. You can't turn it on and off any time you want to. Not if you take pride in yourself."

On the morning that Herb's and Nancy's second child was delivered—mongoloid—Herb had been scheduled to speak before a father and son Communion breakfast at their church. He didn't want to go, but Nancy insisted. Those who were there said Herb spoke without notes, without mentioning what had happened that morning—no one there knew until later. He spoke longer than he usually did. Quietly, he spoke of family, of love, of doing one's best at whatever one does and of accepting what life offers without complaint. He could have been thinking of the damaged daughter who the next day would be christened Susan Jane; he could also have been thinking of an arm that mysteriously died. Those who were there said no talk of Herb's ever moved them more.

---

* In *Baseball When the Grass Was Green* by Donald Hoenig.

Rocky
Bleier

I f you believe in numbers, he should have been a lawyer, maybe an insurance salesman. Because the figures were terrible.

It was January 7, 1968, and teams of the National Football League were choosing the college players they wanted to hire. Rocky Bleier was not at the head of anyone's list. As a matter of fact, he wasn't even on most lists.

With thousands of athletes pouring out of colleges each year, the pros need some orderly way to rate and eventually pick those few, of the thousands, they would like to add to their rosters.

Long before selection time, teams give players points for their weaknesses, their deficiencies. For example, if John Fiercelooking of the University of Wherever can't catch a ball, that's a problem—and he gets a bundle of points. And, months later, when draft time arrives and a team wants to know how it rated John, it asks its computer and out pops a figure. Fiercelooking's football days are over.

The *worst* rating possible is 2.5. Above 1.8, the player "is not capable of playing pro ball." Bleier was judged from 2.2 to 2.4. Wait. It gets worse. One Bleier observer noted: ". . . can't win in the NFL with this kid." Another: "I don't think this boy can make a pro club."

But Rocky had some "intangibles" where the Pittsburgh

Steelers were concerned. Things they couldn't put into the machine. For example, one coach said "heart." Tell that to a computer programmer. So when the Steelers, a club that had won four of 14 games in 1967, got down to the bottom of its computer, that coach raised his voice a little and asked something like, "How do you measure heart?" and Bleier got picked." He was number 417 of 441 men finally selected by the NFL.

The Steelers picked 18 players that year. Bleier, number 18, is the only one still in pro ball.

The army drafted Rocky before his rookie year with Pittsburgh ended and sent him to Vietnam. Nine months later, he was returned: his right foot was a half shoe-size smaller than his left; the bottom of that foot had been ripped open by shrapnel along the instep from heel to ball, across the big toe and the second toe; the second toe was splintered. Dozens of pieces of shrapnel had pierced his right leg from his foot to his thigh.

Bleier, a disarmingly honest man, is equally candid with God. As he lay behind clumps of bushes in South Vietnam, wounded, weapon gone, close enough to the enemy to hear them, well aware their machine gun could cut through the growth and kill him, wondering if his small, cut-off group would be overrun, he prayed: "Dear Lord, get me out of here if you can. I'm not going to bullshit you. I'd like to say that if you get me out of here alive and okay, I'll dedicate my life to you and become a priest. I can't do that because I know that's not what I'll do. I don't want to promise anything now and then change my mind later when things are going good. I don't want to come to you with a tight-situation prayer if I can't be honest. What I will do is this. I'll give you my life . . . to do with whatever you will. . . . I'm not going to complain if things go wrong. If things go good, I'll share my success with everybody around me. Whatever you want to do, wherever you want to direct me, that's fine. This is the best I can do."

A grenade had exploded at Bleier's feet. A steel plate built into army combat boots was the only reason he still had a right foot. Muscle and flesh also had been ripped from his left thigh by small-arms fire.

What are you going to do when you get back to civilian life, Rock?

"I'm a football player, aren't I?"

Well, maybe not. Maybe not when the army lists you officially as 40 per cent disabled. And the disability affects as important a part of you as the sole of a foot. A running back has to start, and push off from, a three-point stance —crouched and leaning on one hand and the toes and balls of both feet. Pushing off is a fundamental move for a runner. It allows him to start quickly and change direction sharply.

Calcium deposits that form around broken bones and scar tissue had, in effect, "frozen" the first two toes and adjacent ligament and muscle areas of Bleier's right foot. The toes would not bend, forward or backward. In addition, muscles on the ball of the right foot had begun to atrophy.

The injuries to the right foot would be Bleier's major obstacle. The other wounds would heal even though infection had invaded as high as his calf. An operation by army surgeons attempted to cut out the scar tissue and bone spurs in the hope it—and later physical therapy—would allow Bleier to regain the flexibility and strength he once had there. The operation was only partially successful. Therapy did little, even electrical stimulation therapy in which a technician shocked the bottom of Bleier's right foot trying to induce movement in his toes was unsuccessful.

Play again?

An army physician in a Tokyo hospital was the first in

line: "Rocky, it's impossible." His old coach at Notre Dame, Ara Parseghian, was next although Ara couldn't bring himself to tell Rocky directly: "He's had half his foot shot away. You need your hip, knee and ankle in perfect shape just to walk. Even with a little blister, you can't run. Here he's had all the ligaments, tendons and muscles damaged. I just hope he'll be able to walk normally."

When the wounds healed, Bleier began to work out by himself. He was on light duty at Fort Riley, Kansas. His injuries looked mended, he thought. So they must *be* mended. He thought he would just jog a couple of miles the first day. An easy, slow start.

At about a half mile, he collapsed, ". . . crying in deep, convulsive sobs as I gasped for air. My mind was racing in disbelief. After all those years as an athlete—my body skilled, strong, responsive—I was now a physical disaster, My foot hurt, my heart was pounding, I couldn't breathe and I lay there, with training camp three months away. Will I ever play football again?"

Bleier *couldn't* run. He couldn't walk. He couldn't put his foot down in any position without extreme pain. He was limping badly. He felt what seemed to be a sharp stone in his right shoe, but he couldn't find it.

Bleier devised an inner-sole device that made it possible to run on that right foot without agony and put himself on a murderous schedule: up at 5:30 A.M. to run outdoors near his off-base apartment, report to his duty assignment at 7:00, lift weights at the post gym from 6:00 to 8:00 P.M., drive back to his apartment, run sprints on the lawn for an hour, shower and go to bed. For five days a week, for three months, that was Bleier's life. He didn't miss an exquisite moment of it.

Bleier ran frequently against roommate Steve Eller, who outweighed Rocky by some 70 pounds. Rocky couldn't beat a man who was not an athlete and who was far from a perfect physical specimen.

"When I did beat the SOB," Rocky told me much later, "it would be by perhaps a step in the 40-yard-dash. And Eller would stick the knife in: 'You're a football player? If I were in shape, I'd beat the ass off you.' He was right. The refrain reverberated within my skull: 'You're an athlete? You're an athlete?' The only way I could 'answer' was to run more."

As Bleier's foot began to hurt less, he and Eller ran up and down the steps at Kansas State University's football stadium, one of the most torturous stunts ever devised for man. Bleier reached the point where he could run up and down, bottom to top, full-out, five consecutive times with 10-pound weights tied to each ankle.

Discharged in July 1970, Bleier moved in with former Notre Dame teammate Terry Hanratty and Terry's wife Rosemary in Pittsburgh. The first NFL player strike was on and Bleier stayed out of preseason training camp with the other Steeler veterans. Hanratty took one look at Bleier and began to worry. ("You're really limping, Rock." "What the hell's the matter with you? I'm not limping.") Hanratty became concerned.

"Rock," he said, "you know the team's a lot different now than it was in '68." (A new coach, Chuck Noll, had been hired in 1969. He was to sweep through the Steeler team that greeted him. Only five were left by Super Bowl time, 1974.)

"Yeah."

Bleier had talked at Notre Dame of becoming a lawyer and Hanratty reminded him. "You've been thinking of law. Take the entrance exams this fall. Maybe you should quit. You sure as hell don't need this."

Rocky didn't get angry. Hanratty was a very close

friend. "I'd like to give it a shot, Terry, and see what happens."

Bleier asked the team veterans at a meeting in early August if he could report to training camp because of his special reconditioning needs and the players agreed. Rocky had only one goal for the '70 season: rejoin the club. He didn't care how he rejoined the team; a spot on the taxi squad would do (that is with the players under contract who practice with the team but aren't included on the official roster and can't play in league games). He didn't care if he played. He didn't want to be "out of sight, out of mind" for two seasons.

Nine running backs were in camp, including Bleier. They were competing for five spots. Dick Hoak and Earl Gros were the only backs remaining from 1968, Rocky's rookie year. Two had joined as rookies in 1969: Warren Bankston of Tulane and Don McCall of Southern California. Two came on trades during the '69–'70 off-season: Frenchy Fuqua from the Giants and Preston Pearson from the Colts.

Training camp is a brutal time, physically and emotionally. Past records mean nothing. The best players make the ball club. It's not a personality contest. It's a vicious battle for a job and even a wounded Vietnam veteran can expect no special consideration. It's cut and dried, black and white.

Bleier's foot was hurting and he was limping steadily. (He thought he was not and could not be persuaded until much later that, in fact, he had limped badly with every step, walking or running, during all of training camp.) He had gotten his weight up from 160 to where it had been, 200, but his speed—rather, lack of it—shook him during the first 40-yard sprints. His best as a rookie in uniform was perhaps 4.8 seconds. His untimed victories in Kansas over Eller had given him false confidence; for he was now, in camp, running close to 6 seconds, out of the question for a pro at *any* spot, even the biggest lineman.

He was running flatfooted, using the outside edge of his right shoe. (He still runs that way today.) He couldn't get up on his toes. The equipment man did what he could. He put a bar under Rocky's right shoe, hoping he could push off that way when starting, rather than use his toes. He removed a cleat from under the big toe on the right foot, hoping to relieve painful pressure on the toe. Nothing worked. Bleier wrapped his right foot in extra tape and socks, especially during exhausting two-a-day practices that drain even the best conditioned players.

Bleier had convinced himself that he was improving, was getting faster, growing stronger, becoming more impressive. All not true. He became the cause of heated debates. Art Rooney, Jr., a vice-president, told his brother Dan, Steelers' president: "The kid's going to get hurt. A back can't be *taking* all the blows. He's got to be *giving* them. Rocky can't protect himself. One of these afternoons when he's really tired, he's going to get killed."

Dr. John Best, the Steelers' orthopedic surgeon, agreed: "He can't go, Danny. He just can't go." From the equipment man: "I can't stand by and watch him go through any more." From the trainer: "Rocky won't quit on his own. It's not human . . . to let him endure any more pain."

Backfield coach Mac Coley spoke privately to Bleier. "Football's just not that important, Rock. It's only a small part of your life. It's not worth it if you're going to be permanently damaged."

Bleier played little during the preseason exhibition games. A week before the season was to start, it was time for the final cut. (NFL teams then could carry 47 players. Hopefuls were eliminated during the preseason training.) Noll sent for Bleier.

Noll's an unemotional pragmatist. The message was blunt. "Rock, we put you on final waivers. We think you'll pass through" (i.e., not be selected by another club). Final waivers offers a player to any club for $100 before his team releases him outright. Clearly, no team would want Bleier if the Steelers didn't. "Get yourself into shape. Then you can come back next year."

Rocky's goal—stay with the club *somehow*—was dying.

Bleier is neither unemotional nor, at that moment, was he outstandingly pragmatic. He argued. "Coach, can't I be sent to the taxi squad or something? I feel good. I can help. I don't want to lose the whole season." Bleier tried for another moment, then turned to leave. What can you say after you've been fired?

"As I began to walk out," Rocky said, "Chuck showed a crack in his impenetrable exterior for the first and only time in my experience. His voice softened a tone and he said, 'If you want, you can practice with us today.'"

Everyone on the team knew Bleier had been cut, yet—a workout was waiting. Rocky Bleier doesn't miss workouts. Even when they're for nothing. He suited up and worked out. Then he left. He was the final man of 25 cut.

Driving home, Bleier was alternately storming and crying. "For the first time since fifth grade, I wasn't a football player any more."

Then a rare force entered Bleier's life. It was a 69-year-old man who had owned a football team for 39 years and never saw it win even a division title. No pro football owner has yet been suggested for sainthood, but Arthur Rooney, Sr., someday will sit at the right hand of St. Peter, cigars and all. I guarantee it.

Bleier received a phone call the morning after he had been cut. Dan Rooney would like to see him. Dan hadn't read the waiver list until late the previous evening. He told his father. His father wondered if another operation on his right foot would help Rocky. Dan, in fact, had suggested that to Bleier at the very start of training camp, but eager to get with the team, Bleier had declined. Dan then asked Noll if he would mind if Bleier were put on the injured reserve list. He couldn't play but he would be with the team unofficially and not take up one of the playing spots. Noll agreed.

When Bleier got to Dan's office, Dan told him of the proposed operation and suggested that Rocky could rejoin the team later in the season after recuperating. Bleier *would* remain a Steeler for the 1970 season.

Surgery was the following day. Dr. Best found and removed a small piece of shrapnel that had worked its way to the surface just below Rocky's fourth toe. That was the "sharp stone" he had been feeling. While Bleier was under anesthesia, Dr. Best with his hands simply ripped scar tissue apart in and around the other toes, freeing them and the ligaments and muscles in the area. Exercise would keep scar tissue from re-forming. For the first time since the grenade exploded, Bleier now had reasonable movement in his right toes.

An anticipated four-week recuperation took eight weeks but only three in bed. Mr. Rooney, Sr., told Art, Jr., to give Bleier some scouting assignments and said, "He might like it. If his foot doesn't get better, let's see if we can find a place for him." An employer owes a returning veteran 30 days work. No more. Bleier had been wounded in the army and his medical problems were the army's responsibility. Mr. Rooney, Sr., paid for the operation and gave Rocky a 25 per cent raise over his rookie salary.

Between infrequent scouting jobs, Bleier began working out on his own. By the eighth week, he was in uniform again, practicing with the team and attending meetings. By the final game of the season, two backs had been hurt and Noll reactivated Rocky so he could get into uniform and sit with the club on the field. Pittsburgh ended the season with five wins and nine losses.

Bleier took an apartment near Chicago, a job selling insurance, and a pledge he would be better when the 1971 season began. Again up at 6:00 to run slush-filled streets; sell insurance from 8:00 until 1:00; weights until 6:00; sell insurance until 9:00; sprints for an hour and bed. Bleier was alone in a new area and his only company was a recurring inner voice: *"Bleier driving over for the touchdown."* Fragile motivation for 6:00 A.M. on a winter's day in Chicago when no one is looking.

His insurance business suffered as Bleier agonized over his right foot and wondered if he could survive a second training camp when he was still far from ideal condition. He called the Steelers to ask if he could report early—with the rookies. He joked about his insurance work. Chuck Noll responded quietly: "Rock, if you've got something good going in Chicago, maybe it would be best if you didn't try to come back."

Bleier pushed away that kindness—and it was that—and received permission to report early. He continued to work out. And then, a week before he was to report, he pulled a hamstring muscle in his left leg just where bullets had cut out a piece of it.

He arrived at camp and, first day, ripped the injured hamstring. Out of action for three weeks. He would miss the most vital part of training camp for the marginal athlete trying to win a team spot—the two-a-day practices. Dr. Best had a talk with Bleier.

"What do you do in the offseason, Rock?"

"I sell insurance."

"Do you like it?"

"Yeah."

"You know, you were wounded in that left thigh. You lost a chunk of your leg. You're always going to have trouble with your hamstrings. I'm going to have to tell Dan and Chuck this. Think about insurance, will you." That last wasn't a question, not the way Dr. Best said it.

Several days later, Noll asked Bleier. "How's it feeling?"

"I don't know," Bleier said. "I think I need a little more time."

"I'm afraid we don't have much time. We have to start making some decisions about people."

Bleier didn't respond.

"Look, Rock, why don't you follow up on your insurance business? I think you should retire."

The team flew to Green Bay for an exhibition game. Bleier drove to his hometown, Appleton, Wisconsin, after the game, talked with his family and visited his old friend and high school counselor, Father Al Lison.

Bleier put out what he believed were his three options: (1) wait for the hamstring to heal completely; by that time, it might be too late in training camp to make the team; (2) continue to practice and pray it wouldn't pull again; and, (3) quit.

"Only one makes sense to me now, Al," he said. "Strap up the leg and go back to practice on Monday. If I pull it again, I pull it and I'm done. If I don't pull it, maybe I've got a chance."

Bleier returned to camp, wrapped the leg, and worked. The final cuts were coming. Five running backs were question marks. One would stay. One more might make the taxi squad. Three would go. His chances were slim.

The team played an exhibition against Cincinnati. One back was cut. An exhibition against Minnesota. Another running back was cut. Bleier was the only back who had not yet played. Then the Jets—and Bleier saw his first action of any kind since his rookie year with the Steelers. He went in halfway through the last quarter. He hurtled through a hole for four yards, scrambled through another for 16, caught a pass for six. A third running back was cut. Of the questionables, Bleier and another man were left.

Rocky then played briefly against the Giants and did little. The following Wednesday was final-cut day. En route home from New York, Bleier began to feel ill. By Pittsburgh, he was sick enough to go directly to a doctor. Acute tonsillitis.

Wednesday morning, Noll called Bleier in. "Rock, we put you on waivers. We think you'll pass through again. Once we see how your throat is, in a game or two, we'll reactivate you."

Bleier was quick-witted enough to say thank you and left. But he wondered. After trying to persuade him weeks earlier to retire, Noll had kept him. Why? Bleier now knew he had not yet shown Noll—anyone—evidence that he was a player to be kept on a club clearly building for a long-time stay at the top. He was upset by whispers that he was not released because he was Irish and from Notre Dame and a medal winner (Bronze Star and Purple Heart).

Limping with the still unhealed hamstring, Bleier heard the whispers and the outright talk and they hurt. He didn't want favors. The standout athlete in elementary school, an 11-letter winner in high school, the *captain* of Notre Dame's football team shouldn't need gifts. Yet he was still somewhat of a caricature of an athlete. Why *did* Noll keep him? "I was something less than a football player. Looking at the situation honestly, what club would have kept me once they saw I was of no immediate use?"

He later learned that backfield coach Max Coley, who the year before had suggested he quit, wanted Bleier. In a coaches' meeting before the '71 season opener against Chicago, Coley said, "Rocky's the only guy I have who will stick his nose in there and block Dick Butkus." When Bleier heard that, he said, "Sure I would have. Hell, that was *all* I could do."

Bleier played that year, eight games, in spite of pulling the injured hamstring again. All on special teams, or as we say in the trade suicide squads (selected athletes who form units solely for such situations as kickoffs, kickoff returns, field goal and extra point tries, punts and punt returns; their number and character vary from team to team). He still was not a player of pro caliber. He was still outside in a way, looking in. I know the feeling well. When you're hurt, when you're not contributing, even if it's only for a game or two, suddenly you're an outsider. These could be—in my case were—athletes you had played with for years, but you're not one of them. It's unspoken. But it's real. And it rubs a raw nerve. That's how Bleier felt during much of that on-again, off-again 1971 season.

But goal number two was accomplished. Bleier now was *on* the team. And that helped. The Steelers finished 6–8.

Back to suburban Chicago, insurance and reconditioning. He had to prove he was a hard-nosed pro who needed no considerations from anyone. The emphasis was on strengthening his right foot. He ignored the ever-present pain in the foot and started racing full-steam up and down the steps of his apartment building. He started with three floors up and down three times without stopping, then four up and down four times, then five, six, seven, eight. Eight floors, full-out, eight times up and down without stopping to die.

He did the stairs routine daily. He returned to his omni-present weights. He added a half-hour to his schedule of the previous offseason. He got up at 5:30 instead of 6:00, squeezed in an afternoon workout as well. So he was now exercising three times a day—six days a week—instead of two. He also ran five 350-yard races daily in less than 60 seconds each and finished each day with sprints. He *had* to move faster, bad foot or not.

He went home for Christmas and discovered his 51-year-old father standing on his head. Bleier's father had taken up yoga and he was far more flexible than his son. Bleier couldn't touch his head to the floor while sitting on the floor; his father could. Rocky was still learning from his father. He bought a beginning yoga book. Perhaps the weight lifting had tightened his muscles, particularly in his legs. Would flexibility exercises added to the ever-present weight lifting and the running help?

He found out first day back at 1972 training camp. Everyone was being timed at 40-yard dashes. Three watches clicked and off went Bleier. He trotted back to find three coaches shaking their watches next to their ears, listening for broken parts. Bleier had been timed *faster* than his rookie year. One watch had 4.55. The slowest had 4.65—two-tenths of a second faster than he was before he was wounded. (This just shouldn't happen. Gil Brandt, the Dallas Cowboys' director of personnel, put it well. "No one ever gets faster in pro football," he once said. "You pick up a back who runs a 4.8 and maybe in a few years he'll be 4.9 and a few years later he'll be 5.0 and too slow to play.")

Why was Rocky faster? The foot still hurt.

Three years of work were beginning to pay off for the tough kid who wasn't supposed to be able to play pro ball when he was whole, was told to quit when he was wounded, and wasn't smart enough to listen to anyone. Three years of building strength into his legs and body, the extensive winter, spring and early summer of flexibility exercises —courtesy of Mr. Bleier, Sr.—and another intangible: he *wanted* to be faster.

"No question that by the offseason between '71 and '72 I was overcompensating," Bleier said. "I was studying sprinters' form to see how they ran, their arms, their legs, position of their feet. My own workouts almost daily pushed me beyond what I had thought my limits to be. I probably could have done half of what I did and improved my speed by 1972, but I didn't know that."

Goal number three was to play in '72. To show everyone he was there on his own merit. He did play—every game. By the time the year ended, with the Steelers 11–3 and a division winner for the first time in their history, Bleier was established—but only on special teams.

The fact that Bleier played every game didn't satisfy him. Bleier wanted to be a starter. He had carried the ball once during the season.

In the next offseason, in what had come to be Bleier's trials by self-imposed ordeals, he decided to build up his strength and bulk. Back to six days a week. Running and weight lifting continued. He began talking with professional body builders and picking their brains. He used the help also of two coaches Pittsburgh had just hired: Lou Riecke, a strength coach, and Paul Uram, a flexibility coach.

During the '72 season, following his yoga workouts, Rocky went through his first football season without injury. With Uram, the team's number of muscle pulls and serious leg injuries was cut by more than half. Bleier visited a physiologist and learned ways to better develop his leg muscles that a cutting, dodging, accelerating running back needs most. Bleier's weight rose to 225, then slimmed to 216 rock-solid pounds when training camp for 1973 began.

This was the year, Bleier had told himself, in which he would "make" the team on his terms, as a running back.

His condition was superb. The team equipment manager changed his shoulder pads; Bleier was two sizes larger than as a rookie. Only two men on the team—both offensive linemen—were stronger than Bleier. Only two were faster: wide receiver Frank Lewis and running back Steve Davis.

During the exhibition games, Rocky now was running.

He led all the backs in average yards-per-carry when the season began. But during the final exhibition game, he hurt his knee. By the time his knee mended, Franco Harris, Pittsburgh's number-one runner who also had been hurt, was back. Bleier returned to special teams.

He played on all six teams—kickoff and punt coverage, kickoff and punt return, field goal, and extra-point kicking. He was gaining fame as special-teams player. He was usually the first Steeler downfield and—blocking or tackling—used his body in more ways than nature intended. Television directors turned isolated cameras on him: Look what Bleier did now, folks.

But he remained the fifth and last running back in Noll's mind. Near the end of the year, Noll wanted better blocking on third downs and short yardage, on third and scoring position. He asked Dick Hoak, who had returned to the Steelers as backfield coach, who his best blocker was. Bleier, said Hoak, also mentioning—apparently unheard—that Bleier runs with the ball, too.

So Bleier went in perhaps six to eight times a game, usually to block, sometimes to carry, and was uncomfortable. "Not only are you coming in cold; you haven't been in long enough to know what the other team is doing; you put your reputation on the line during just a fraction of a game. Specialty teams are different; that's sort of a game within a game and it has its own 'rules.'" The Noll experiment soon ended.

The Steelers, picked by some as the dark horse favorite of the year, finished with 10–4 and a spot in the playoffs. Oakland eliminated them in the first game.

The following season, 1974, the year Pittsburgh was to win in the Super Bowl, began with Bleier beginning to think of himself as a journeyman ballplayer, one whom Noll considered only in terms of special teams.

The Players Association started the 1974 training camp

by calling a strike. The Steelers' team representative had resigned. Preston Pearson succeeded and asked Bleier to help. He agreed. It didn't help his image. "After what the Rooneys did for him, how could he turn on them?" Even Rocky's mother had a few tart words.

Art Rooney, Sr., heard the criticism and called Bleier: "Rock, I heard someone question your allegiance to the Rooneys. He said you owed us more loyalty than you're showing during this strike because we supposedly 'carried' you after your Vietnam experience. I just want to tell you that's not true. You've been an asset to us, both on and off the field. We don't want you to think you owe us anything. If you feel what you're doing is right, that's fine with me."

(Mr. Rooney is, by the way, remarkable. On the last day of the 1963 season, the Giants were playing the Steelers. Pittsburgh, which had had so many lean years, needed a tie or a win to take its first division title ever. It was the third quarter. We were leading, 16–10, but Pittsburgh now was dominating the play. We took possession deep in our own territory and moved to our 24-yard-line.

On third down, Y.A. Tittle called a pass pattern that would take me down and in. The ball was ahead of me and I had to leap just across midfield. I stuck out one hand and the ball astonishingly stuck. It was amazing luck—and the biggest catch I ever made. Two plays later, Joe Morrison scored, the momentum turned and we won, 33–17. In our locker room after the game, Mr. Rooney, cigar in mouth, unnoticed by reporters, came over to me and congratulated me warmly on the catch.)

Bleier began to be assailed by doubts. It was, of course, possible that he was wrong and everyone else right. Should he quit? Should he keep to his torturous workouts? Were they going to get him somewhere? Bleier realized that at 28 he was getting old as far as special teams are concerned. He could easily be replaced by a rookie. And, because he now had five years in for a league pension, the club could consider him expendable.

During the exhibition period, Bleier was reduced to two specialty teams: kickoff and kick return. He logged minimal time as a running back. Franco Harris and Steve Davis started all the exhibition games.

The same pair started the season as running backs. Pittsburgh defeated Baltimore and tied with Denver. Harris hurt his leg. Frenchy Fuqua took over. The Steelers lost to Oakland.

A new running-back unit was formed in the last five minutes of the first half against Houston the next week. The Steeler offense was sputtering. Noll sent Bleier and Pearson in. The Steelers moved 39 yards and scored a field goal.

Bleier and Pearson started the second half. Bleier's blocking was superb. He gained 37 yards. Pearson ran for 117. Pittsburgh won, 13–7.

Kansas City was next; Noll stayed with his new running combination. It was Bleier's first start in the NFL. Pittsburgh won again, 34–24. Bleier scored his first touchdown. He gained 45 yards running and 45 more on pass receptions. He was the Steelers' high man in total offense.

Pearson and Bleier started against Cleveland the following week. The Steelers won their third consecutive game.

Now Harris was ready to play again. Bleier had been playing Franco's position, fullback. Noll moved Rocky to halfback in spite of the fact that he had not run a play from halfback all season. Bleier would start with Harris against Atlanta.

That game proved to be the pivotal one of the season for the Steelers and for Bleier. The offense—including a line that had been changing from week to week as the coaching staff sought the best combination—finally jelled. Harris and Bleier both set career highs rushing, Franco, 141 yards, and Rocky, 78. (To put that 78-yard total in perspective, Bleier had gained only 70 yards total, including his 1968 rookie year, until that game.) Bleier scored one of Pittsburgh's three touchdowns.

His blocking was deadly efficient. It was to be instrumental in helping Harris gain 881 yards running in the last nine regular season games and 512 yards and six touchdowns in the playoffs.

Many things went into Bleier's blocking success: his strength, courtesy of all those offseasons spent lifting weights; his leverage because he was smaller than most everyone on the field; and his desire, articulated at Notre Dame by assistant coach Tom Pagna: "Blocking is just a lot of wanting to." Noll began to call Bleier his "third guard."

Franco and Rocky started again the following week and the Steelers shut out Philadelphia. Against Cincinnati, Rocky pulled the Achilles tendon in his left foot. The Steelers lost. Bleier sat out much of the next two games. Pittsburgh defeated Cleveland again, then New Orleans. Bleier thought he was back on the bench to stay. Houston followed and the offense fell apart. Bleier went back in. Pittsburgh lost, 13–10, the last game it was to lose in 1974. Bleier stayed in the lineup as Pittsburgh defeated New England and Cincinnati.

Against Buffalo in the first playoff game, he gained 99 yards running and receiving as the Steelers won, 32–14. A 27-yard touchdown pass, Bradshaw to Bleier, put Pittsburgh in front to stay in the second quarter, 10–7. Oakland was next and lost to the Steelers, 24–13. Harris ran for 111 yards and Bleier gained only 13 less rushing and 25 on passes. (As late in the season as that game, football writers noted "surprise" at Bleier's play.) The game's turning point came early in the fourth quarter when Pittsburgh drove 61 yards in nine plays to tie the score. All but one of those plays were on the ground by Harris and Bleier. Bleier's 23-yard run was the longest in that series.

The 1975 and 1976 Super Bowls were anticlimactic for Bleier. His running and blocking were parts of a superb machine that manhandled Minnesota in 1975 and defeated Dallas in 1976. Recall the point system I mentioned earlier by which teams judged prospects? Of the starting Pittsburgh team in both Super Bowls, no one had been rated as poorly as Bleier. His fellow backs, for example, Terry Bradshaw and Franco Harris, were 0.9 and 1.0, respectively, As far as anyone can predict anything in football, Bleier will be an important man with that club for years to come.

Monuments. The world is filled with things built to honor this event or that person. Someone might make a case for "monuments" within people. Bleier is a monument, to me, of the kind of God-given intensity some fools call stupidity. Out of the debris that was Bleier in 1970 emerged a running back on a twice world championship football team. And no one except Bleier anticipated that. Who said God doesn't talk to Notre Dame men?

Charley
Boswell

Charley Boswell lost his sight about 130 days after he had signed a pro baseball contract. He was a tall, handsome young athlete who could get the fat part of his bat on any pitch devised by man—and it all became nothing in the rubble near a small German town when Charley jumped into a burning tank to pull out an injured soldier.

The tank was under fire from machine guns. It was about to blow and an infantry captain shouldn't have been worrying about it in the first place, but he went. Boswell leaped from the safety of a roadside ditch when he saw the tankman get hit and fall back inside the hulk. He squeezed his six-foot bulk through a hatch, shoved the wounded man out and onto the road and then hoisted himself up to the rear deck. That's when the shell hit—a fraction of a second before Charley would have been off the tank and back into his ditch.

He was given up for dead and it wasn't until that evening when the town was secure and the grave detail came to get the dead that they found Boswell. Shrapnel from the shell that had exploded at his feet had made a mess of him. The most serious wounds were to his eyes. For three months physicians in hospitals in Germany, France, England and the United States kept his hopes alive as they operated nine times—and waited to see if vision would return.

Finally, at a military hospital near Philadelphia, the doctors realized they were chasing rainbows and told Charley.

What does a man whose life had been sports since elementary school do at a time like that? What does he do with that pro contract calling him to play for Paul Richards' famed Atlanta Crackers?

Boswell, understandably, went into mourning. There was plenty of reason. He had been an all-state and all-southern athlete in high school. He had come to the University of Alabama before the war started in Europe—it was about the time Bear Bryant signed on there as an assistant coach—and did just about everything in Alabama's backfield. He was a triple-threat athlete. Remember that term? It was a phrase in vogue before the age of specialists reached football. Boswell's punting record at Alabama stood until 1972. So there was football to mourn. Baseball, too. Boswell was a superb centerfielder and he was drawing a bead, the New York Yankee scouts pursuing him said, on Joe DiMaggio's job with the Yankees.

And, of course, there was his family. Certainly not least. There was Kitty whom he had married just before he had been drafted and there was their daughter Kay, a year old. How, Charley wondered, does a blind man support a family?

But he wanted to adapt and so he went to lectures the army had worked out for men like him. You can guess what they were like: "The war's over for you, son, and unfortunately you've got to make some serious adjustments." Charley also signed up for the hospital's recreational therapy program.

He tried bowling, a sport in which he had done very well before the war. Only now, his follow-through carried him under the ball rack with his ball bouncing three alleys away. And he went horseback riding—to be knocked off his horse when it bolted under a low tree limb.

Gradually, he dropped out of one hospital activity after another. He couldn't fake enthusiasm. He knew he would have to think about earning a living for himself and his family, but he couldn't keep himself in rehabilitation. The one goal that had motivated him from childhood—sports— was gone and he didn't know quite what to replace it with. He was 22—and terrified.

"Before long, I was spending my days in my hospital room listening to the talking-book machine or the radio," he was to tell me years later. "I wouldn't join in anything. I wouldn't talk to anyone. I wouldn't see anyone. I was on my way to becoming a vegetable."

The strength of two dedicated men brought him back to the world he had to cope with. One was a stranger and the other, as close to Boswell as a brother. One was dedicated to helping wounded men regain the pattern of life. The other man was dedicated to Charley Boswell. One remained with him for three months; the other, for 28 years.

Corporal Ken Gleason was the first. He walked into Boswell's hospital room a week or two after Boswell had learned he would be permanently blind and invited him out for a game of golf.

The reaction could have been predicted. Men who walk the streets with white canes don't play golf.

"Get the hell out of here," Boswell replied coldly, furious at what he interpreted as someone's black humor. He ordered the corporal from the room.

Gleason held firm. A golfer for many years and a member of the hospital's recreation staff, he saw no reason golf had to be restricted to those who could see. He sat and waited for Boswell to run down. Then he asked again— and pushed a little. Finally, Boswell went along, to get rid of him, he was to say. ("One swing and he'd take me back.") Charley, who had thrived on team sports, had never been on a golf course. Kitty had once asked him to play with her and he had refused; golf just wasn't his game.

Gleason drove Boswell to a nearby course. For about a half-hour, he told Boswell how to hold and swing a club. Then they walked over to the practice area.

Gleason pulled out a 2-wood, teed up the ball, set the club head behind it, adjusted Charley's stance slightly and then stepped back.

"Go ahead," he said.

Boswell swung and as he hit the ball, he felt the same kind of impact he had known in baseball when he connected solidly with a pitch.

"Where'd it go?" he asked.

"The ball's about 200 yards down the fairway," Gleason said. "Right in the middle. It was a beautiful shot."

Black humor again, Boswell thought. Grimly: "Gleason, don't lie to me."

"It's right where I said it is, Captain. We can walk out there if you want to."

Boswell was quiet for a moment, then asked if he could try another one. He hit 10. Nine landed on the fairway at least 200 yards from the tee.

"Let's try a few holes," Gleason suggested.

They played four holes that afternoon, returned each of the next 10 days for nine and two weeks later Boswell played his first full round of 18 holes.

During the next few months, as he was mending sufficiently to be discharged, Boswell learned how to play golf when he could see neither ball nor hazard nor undulating green. He played with a coach, Gleason. The young soldier guided Boswell on foot around the course, each holding an end of a club. He told Boswell where the ball was, selected the proper club and aligned its face with the ball. He adjusted Boswell's stance by moving the club until it and Boswell were positioned correctly.

Boswell learned that golf, for the blind, required an absolutely grooved swing. This meant his basic game had to be sound. Without sight, he could not adapt a swing to meet the requirements of an individual shot. He could do a certain amount of letting out or holding back but that was all. Each shot—wood, iron or putt—was a straight one for Boswell.

When he reached a green, Boswell linked arms with Gleason and paced off the distance to the cup. Gleason made allowance for the location of the cup and the condition of the green by telling Charley, for example, to shoot as if for a three-footer when the green was fast and the pin was really six or eight feet away.

A natural athlete gifted with excellent coordination, Boswell soon was shooting in the 90s. Sports had reentered his life. Golf would not allow him to support his family, but his success at it was the first positive thing that happened to him since he had been wounded.

Still, golf then was merely exercise to Boswell. When he returned to his native Birmingham, Alabama, he felt he was just drifting. He became a salesman for the sporting-goods section of a local department store—and soon was the unit's manager—but he wasn't used to the absence of a vital part of his old life, always preparing for a new test. "In every athlete's mind," Knute Rockne once wrote, "there is always the thought 'what's next, what's the next achievement?' " Boswell was still a man who was blind and "far from adjusted to life in the dark, a life without competition."

Fighting panic in those first months after his army discharge—panic at being dependent, panic at others' too-evident pity—Boswell refused to take anything the easy way. During the first few days of his job in downtown Birmingham, Kitty drove him.

Then he insisted he go alone. "It was easy," he said. "Three curbstones bump under your feet and you know you're at the trolley line. You hear the trolley and you walk out and get on. When you begin the downgrade, that's the ballpark. The double bang of the trolley going over a track intersection means you're at the car barn on Third Avenue. You smell bread and you're passing a certain bakery. Fumes soon tell you you're coming to the gas works at 14th Street. From there, you count the bang of 18 trolley intersections and we're at my corner."

Charley fought for work that would push the limits blindness had imposed on him. He had a number of pine trees around his home; needles and cones collected in the rain gutters. A neighbor helped Boswell put up a ladder. Charley scrambled onto the roof and cleaned out all the gutters quickly.

But each of these were "simple" tasks, jobs that, once accomplished, had no more challenge to a man searching for a way to return some meaning to his life.

Then Grant Thomas returned to Birmingham from the navy. Thomas had been Boswell's closest friend from childhood. When a hip broken during a high school football game mended, Charley's physician suggested he run track. Grant built starting blocks for Charley to practice with at home. Charley won the state title in the 100-yard dash that year and placed second in the 220. When Alabama's football team went to New York to take on then-powerful Fordham in Yankee Stadium, Thomas followed by bus to watch his friend play. Grant had introduced Charley to Kitty.

Now Thomas was back and Boswell needed him again. A good golfer before the war, Thomas had often tried vainly to get Charley to play. Now it was Boswell who asked Thomas out for a round of golf. Thomas laughed, as an old friend could.

The following day, he became Boswell's coach.

Several months later, Boswell's life regained the purpose he had been seeking since that fall morning in Germany. He was invited to play in what turned out to become the first U.S. National Blind Golf Tournament. Boswell would have competition again. He would again be able to pit himself against equals in a sporting event.

Thomas and the tournaments for blind golfers were to change Boswell's life. During the next 28 years, Thomas and Boswell were to play most of the finest golf courses in the country. These two men developed a relationship I have never seen duplicated in any area of life.

Grant pretty much gave up his own game to help his friend. He picked Boswell up most mornings at 5:30 so Boswell could hit 300 golf balls before they had to go to their jobs. They squeezed in 18 holes after work, then finished under lights with another 300 drives. Grant put Boswell through hundreds of hours of practice with every club.

Grant for a time traveled in his work; when tournaments drew near, he would drive for days to Birmingham to get Charley ready for competition. He timed his vacations to the annual tournaments. Thomas insisted he and Boswell wear matching outfits during tournaments because "we're a team."

Boswell never asked for this kind of devotion, but Grant gave it.

"We can be the best," he said.

Four men competed in the first blind golfers tournament in Los Angeles. The force behind the tournament was Clint Russell, who had been a golfer before he lost his sight in an accident. Russell, who died in 1961, had started golf for the blind years before in his native Duluth, Minnesota.

Boswell was paired with Russell for the first round of the 36-hole competition. Russell had been playing golf blinded for 18 years; Boswell, about 18 months. On the first hole,

Boswell reached the green in two. Russell's second shot landed in a bunker to the right of the green. He blasted it out and into the cup *for a birdie three*. That was Boswell's baptism in the National Blind Golf Tournament.

"Good lord," Boswell asked Grant. "Can Russell see?"

"I don't know, but Ben Hogan couldn't have made that shot any better."

Boswell finished second to Russell in the tournament. Bing Crosby, a fine golfer himself who watched the play, predicted Boswell would win the tournament the next year. And he did.

The competition the second year was held on Russell's home course near Duluth, Minnesota. It would be three rounds, the first two medal play and the last match play.

Charley won the first two rounds with a total of 218 for a 13-stroke lead over Russell. But the winner of the final match play round would win the title.

Boswell held a one-hole advantage at the end of nine. Russell won the 10th and 11th holes to lead by one. They were even on 12, 13 and 14. Boswell won the 15th to tie with Russell.

Russell reached the 16th green in three. On his first bad shot of the tournament, Boswell hooked his approach to the fairway of an adjacent hole. Between him and the green where Russell's ball lay: 150 yards, a tall stand of trees and a cavernous trap. Boswell's 6-iron shot felt good to him. It should have; it stopped two feet from the cup. He dropped the putt for a par four. Russell bogied and Boswell again led by one, now with two holes to go.

Charley drilled in a 13-foot putt for a par three on 17— Russell bogied—and became the new National Blind Golf champion. It was the first of an incredible 17 U.S. titles he would go on to win—with no other blind golfer yet close— and 11 more international championships.

Boswell needed that first title in 1947 far more than anyone realized. It was three years since he had been blinded, but he was still lost, still groping in a world suddenly made strange to him. How *does* one adjust to blindness after 22 years of sight? Boswell, out of the depth of his gut, refused to learn Braille, refused a Seeing Eye dog, refused to wear dark glasses. *He* was still independent. He would do things his way. The world yields only to those who conquer her, Winston Churchill was to tell us, but how can you conquer something you don't see? You can, of course, but Charley Boswell in 1944, 1945 and 1946 didn't think so. Blind men don't compete. So he believed.

Then Charley won that title in Duluth. Suddenly, he understood that blind men and women are more like you and me than they are different. Blindness, he realized, could be "an inconvenience, not a handicap."

"All the time I was playing golf during these three years before Duluth," he told me, "I was really fighting hard in another competition—a personal struggle to find a way to cope with life."

Boswell knew he had to wage that fight on his own terms. The army had wanted him to work in the hospital as a rehabilitation counselor. The salary was $100 a week, fine pay then, but he turned it down to work in the department store for a third of that. Intuitively, Charley knew he had to compete if he was to survive emotionally.

The tournament victory returned Boswell to a degree of normalcy. Nothing would change his blindness, but the world *was* the same one he had known. The familiar thrill of honing a skill and then winning with it against equals restored his confidence in himself. The world no longer seemed quite so strange. He could compete and he could win.

The new confidence led him, in time, to leave the department store to start a retail shoe business of his own. It failed—but he didn't. He opened an insurance office; Kitty read the incredibly complex and varied rate tables to him as he memorized them. His secretary handled the paper work.

The same drive that had been demonstrated in his career at Alabama and in baseball, that had brought him to the head of his class at Officers Candidate School at Fort Benning, Georgia, that had made him request combat after his commission led him to success in business.

"I wanted the closest thing to ballplaying in my daily work," he was to reflect to me. "I *needed* to compete. Foolish after I had lost my sight? Perhaps. But I had to learn if I could support my family in business. That was the most difficult competition I could think of at the time."

The United States Blind Golf Association was formed the following year. Today twenty-four golfers belong. Several are former servicemen blinded in Vietnam. About half had played golf before they lost their sight. Its members conform to *all* U.S. Golf Association regulations with one minor exception. "The game is there to be played on golf's own terms," says Boswell. "The rules of golf can't change to accommodate anyone's personal handicap, no matter what it is." Par is the same for blind golfers as for the sighted. Prospective members must submit a statement from an ophthalmologist certifying total blindness. They must shoot less than 135 for 18 holes. Each player must bring his own coach to tournaments. Sites vary from year to year. Expenses of each player and coach are paid by sponsors, usually civic organizations. The tournaments raise money for groups that help the blind.

I have watched these men play and I have seen firsthand their impact on both the sighted and blind men and women who come to watch their tournaments. The sighted take away with them different ideas about the blind—new understanding of what they can do as well as an increased respect and admiration. An impressive number of the blind spectators are inspired to become more active in life. Charley has told me of many who have found an outlet in sports and recreation —whatever it may be—after attending one of the blind golfers' tournaments.

Boswell and other blind golfers periodically play with members of the pro golf tour who agree to be blindfolded. Only one pro has lasted as many as three holes; he finally quit, pleading nausea to Boswell in apparent truth after continually scrambling for his ball in the rough. He did, Thomas told Boswell, "look rather green."

Boswell has a standing offer open to any sighted golfer to play him blindfolded. Bob Hope once challenged Boswell to a game. "Okay," replied Boswell, "but I pick the course and the time. My club—at midnight." Hope smiled and changed the subject. Some years back, Boswell was to play with a blindfolded Francis Ouimet, who came out of obscurity in 1913 to upset England's outstanding professionals Harry Vardon and Ted Ray and win the U.S. Open.

The match was held in Augusta, Maine. The first hole was a difficult par four with a line of trees and a sharp fall sloping to a rocky creek at the left. Boswell's tee shot was straight down the fairway. Ouimet hooked into the gulch. As his coach began to lead him down the slope, Ouimet fell, swore, ripped off his blindfold and ended the "match." Didn't even pick up his ball.

After a losing streak in '62–'63, Boswell bounced back to take three consecutive blind golfers' tournaments going into the 1966 competition at Stumpy Lakes Golf Course near Norfolk, Virginia. He was then president of the USBGA.

The tournaments had become two rounds of medal play. Boswell finished the first 18 holes with 96—to learn he was second to Canadian Claude Pattemore's 94. Pattemore's spirited coach, Jock McCullough, who had been working with blind golfers for 20 years, told the favored Boswell, "We'll play even better tomorrow and we'll get you."

As association president, Boswell made the daily pairings. He could have played with one of the weaker entrants to ease the pressure on himself; instead, he bracketed himself with Pattemore. Why did he pick the hardest way to win? "If I lose," Boswell said, "he'll have to beat me head to head."

Pattemore led by five strokes at the end of four holes. Boswell then settled down and shot par on seven of the next 10 holes; he birdied one of them and bogeyed the remaining two. He was shooting for an 18-hole 84 until he got into the rough on 17 and 18. He finished with 92 and a three-stroke edge over Pattemore for the title.

Competition among the blind golfers is as fierce as it is in any game sighted men play. "If it doesn't matter if you win or lose but how you play the game, why do they keep score?" Boswell asks.

The day he arrived at the hospital in this country from Europe, Boswell received a call that Kitty would be there the following afternoon. He also was to meet with the hospital's chief of ophthalmology in the morning. "That night," he said, "was a thousand hours long." He dreaded both meetings. His own precariously held hope for a return of vision was waning. Kitty had been told nothing of the nature of his eye wounds, only that he had been hurt around the face and body.

Early the next morning, he saw the physician. When the examination was finished, he told Charley, "Boswell, everything possible has been tried to restore your vision. Nothing more can be done. I'm sorry, but you'll never see again."

Boswell listened numbly as the physician dictated his findings to a secretary. The left eye showed some degree of atrophy. Some atrophy had occurred in the right eye, its cornea was damaged and its optic nerve was severed. "Any one of those conditions could mean blindness," Boswell said. "I had them all."

The physician started telling Boswell "about all the things a person without sight could do." Charley interrupted him. "You don't have to worry about me," he said. "I'd like to go back to my room."

When Kitty arrived, Boswell still hadn't decided how to tell her. He had rented a room for Kitty in a nearby town and they were driven there for dinner, Boswell in a borrowed uniform. He still wore a number of bandages, including one over each eye. Throughout the evening, he groped for a way to tell Kitty what he had learned that morning. He could not.

"When we got back to the house where Kitty was staying," Boswell said, "I sat down in a big chair. Kitty came over and sat in my lap. I didn't want to say anything for a while and just held her. Finally, she said, 'Why don't you tell me about it? It won't make any difference. I know you won't be able to see again.'"

She had told *him*. The tears then began for both of them but "when that was washed out of our system, both of us seemed to realize there was nothing more to be said on the subject. I doubt if we have talked about it for more than a few seconds at a time during the next 30 years."

"Looking back," Boswell was to say, ". . . I realize that Kitty and I were at a crossroads that night as we sat in the big chair . . . , trying our best to comfort each other. I could have gone straight down from there. It would have been easy. But . . . since Kitty believed in me, I had to try to believe in myself."

Several days later, Boswell's parents brought Kay to join them. The child jumped out of the car at a wobbly run to meet her father, sensed that something was wrong, stopped short several feet away from him, turned, and raced back to her grandfather.

"For the next few days, I tried every approach in the book to win her over," Boswell said. "All of them failed. . . . She warmed toward me very gradually, but her full acceptance of me—and of my being 'different'—didn't come without real heartache."

Before Boswell was discharged, Kitty learned she was pregnant again. Neither of them was prepared for that. "I found it hard to bear the thought of having a child I would never be able to see," Boswell said. "At least I could treasure Kay's face from the pictures Kitty had sent me."

Four years later, Boswell was sure enough of himself for Kitty and him to decide to have a third child. He now knew he could handle the responsibility—and that the joy of parenthood could be taken in through all the senses, not solely sight.

Boswell today plays most of the time with sighted players. He joins foursomes at home, plays as quickly as his companions, usually is the first to get a little side bet going and roars when he wins. His blindness can cause *some* problems. Thomas and Boswell were playing in a Lighthouse for the Blind benefit in San Antonio when Charley hit into the rough. Grant had him lined up to shoot when he yelled, "Come on!" Boswell knew that Thomas had left him and was calling as he walked away. Boswell remained, wondering what Thomas' problem was. "Come on, you fool," Thomas yelled again. Boswell casually walked over to Grant and inquired politely about his hysteria. There had been a rattlesnake about six inches from Boswell's club head.

Boswell averages 92, a score better than nine out of ten sighted weekend golfers. His best score for 18 holes is 81, repeated several times on different courses. He often plays in pro-amateur or pro-celebrity tournaments—usually one-day events that raise money for charity or rounds that precede tournaments on the professional golf circuit.

In the Music City Pro-Celebrity Tournament in Nashville

two years ago, he shot 87—with a 39 on the back side—and received a standing ovation from 15,000 spectators as he holed out. He shot 87 again at Music City last year, playing as always from the pro tees.

At the Colonial Country Club in Fort Worth in 1972, Boswell chipped a 30-footer over a pond into the cup on the ninth hole. Caught in sand four times during that round, he got out to make par all but once. His score: 90.

In the Colonial in 1970, Boswell's second shot lifted over a water hazard on the ninth hole, but spun back in. Boswell took a drop and a penalty stroke and, lying four, put his ball 30 feet to the left of the pin. The green was extremely fast. He sank the putt.

Then he really got good. On the par-four 16th hole, his second shot fell into a trap to the right of the pin. The green had two levels with the cup on the lower one. Boswell blasted out and landed six feet from the hole, but on the upper level. His coach aimed Charley four feet to the left of the hole to allow for the break, told him to stroke as easily as he would for a one-foot putt. Boswell put it in for par. He duplicated the par on the very next hole after again hitting his approach into a trap. He calmly blasted out and dropped an uphill, twisting 14-foot putt.

Touring pro Bob Goalby, a good friend who was playing with Boswell, shook his head after Charley finished on the 17th hole and said, "Not one man on the pro tour could do what you just did twice in succession."

Boswell played in 1973 at the Norwood Hills Country Club in St. Louis in an event to raise money for a cystic fibrosis research hospital. The course is exceptionally hilly. On the par-three second hole, 180 yards and water seemingly everywhere, Charley's drive hit 10 inches short of the hole. He dropped it for a birdie two while the pro he was playing with just stared.

I watched Charley in a recent round. He finished with 91, a

score a lot of the guys I play with at Winged Foot, my own course, would like to have, myself included. On the par-three first hole, he reached the green in two and dropped a 14-foot putt. He parred the second, a 509-yard par five, when he two-putted, double-bogeyed the third and parred the fourth.

He birdied an extremely long and tight par-five hole. Natural forest bordered both sides of a good part of the fairway. Two fine wood shots covered more than 400 yards and put the ball just off the front edge of the green. The pin was 30 feet away, uphill, and perhaps five feet in front of a huge, high-walled bunker.

If his chip was too long, the ball could easily land in the trap. His coach told him to hit as if the pin were 20 feet away. The ball stopped two feet short of the cup and Charley holed it for a birdie.

He hit every shot that day cleanly. Few went astray. Charley doesn't miss a ball six times a year. One 40-foot chip shot rolled right over the lip of the cup. He averaged about 215 yards with his woods.

Charley and his coach carried on a running conversation: "You're on the edge of the high grass." "That's not a good lie; you're in clover about ball high." "You're about 45 yards from the flag." "That's great; you landed 15 feet from the pin." "It's an uphill shot; you'll have to add a little bit to it." During all this, Charley cracked bad jokes and swore occasionally.

Like all blind golfers, Charley uses an ordinary set of clubs. He replaced the 2- and 3-irons with a 5- and 6-wood.

Grant Thomas, the extraordinary friend who was not only coach but cheerleader when Boswell got into slumps, died in 1973.

In noting Grant's death, a mutual friend of Boswell and Thomas wrote in the local paper: "Charley was never anything but a blind man on the golf course without Grant Thomas at his side. If Charley Boswell shot 98, then Grant Thomas had done 98 deep knee bends. And he had told Charley Boswell 98 times where the ball went. And he had selected a club 98 times. And if Charley Boswell hit 300 practice balls, then that's 300 times Grant Thomas had bent down and placed the club behind the ball. This went on for 28 years . . . many times on cold, wet and dark mornings.

". . . Ironically, the 58-year-old Thomas died in New Orleans, the scene of their last competition together, the National Blind Golf Tournament at the New Orleans Country Club. Boswell . . . was beaten on the third hole of a sudden-death playoff after Thomas coached him to an incredible final-round 91 in the face of . . . winds that gusted to 50 miles an hour.

" 'Well, we showed 'em two old guys could still play,' Grant cracked wearily to his 'boss.' 'We'll get 'em next year in Boston.'

". . .Most of Boswell's fantastic 28 tournament victories came with Grant Thomas at his side. 'He was just as satisfied, or just as disgusted, with every shot we hit,' said Boswell. Note the use of the pronoun 'we.'

"Wherever Charley got, Grant's work and his love for his friend got him there."

There is no way to tell Boswell is blind when you're with him in a group of people. His conversation is sprinkled with the same "Good to see you" or "We saw a movie the other night" comments all of us make. During the football season I met up with Charley at a multiple sclerosis function in Birmingham. Although I had heard it before, it startled me when Charley casually commented that "he had enjoyed seeing me" on a recent Monday Night Football telecast. He is more self-sufficient than many sighted adults I know. He has a remarkable memory for voices, can dial a phone as fast as I can—he counts the digit holes—and dictates to his secretary from memory better than I do with a handful of notes.

When Charley was working in the department store, a stranger came in one day to get the telephone number of a former employee. When Boswell gave it to him, the man said, "I don't see so well; I left my glasses at home. Will you dial the number for me?" Charley then dialed the number for the man, got the party on the phone, and gave the phone to the visitor. The man then left, still unaware Boswell was blind.

On one trip to New York City, Boswell and I jumped into a cab as the driver held the door open. As we drove off, he heard me talk to Charley about his blindness, pulled over to the side, turned around, looked squarely at Boswell and asked, "*You're* blind?" Charley said he was and we drove off again. About 10 minutes later, Charley started telling me of his most recent golf game. The cab jerked to a stop in a lane of traffic. Our friendly cabbie turned again and demanded, "You play golf?" Charley acknowledged he did. The driver looked incredulous, finally sighed, and turned around. "Well, I know how you feel when you play. I'm lousy, too." "What *do* you shoot?" Boswell asked. "Almost broke a hundred last time." I didn't have the heart to tell the driver that Charley had finished with 88 in a match the day before.

I stayed with Charley and Kitty during a recent visit to Birmingham. It's Charley's custom to prepare breakfast and bring it to Kitty in their bedroom. He made two trays while I was there and brought one to me. "Nothing unusual," he told me. "I do it for everyone who stays with us."

As we drove around Birmingham, its suburbs and countryside, Charley gave me a running commentary on sights we were passing. His timing was never off.

He is extraordinarily popular in Birmingham and in Alabama. His home course, the Highland Park Golf Course, was renamed after him some years back and, in 1974, an annual Charley Boswell Celebrity Tournament was started to raise funds for the Eye Foundation Hospital in Birmingham. The competition raised $25,000 for the hospital in 1974, $30,000 in 1975.

I've shared many head tables at charitable functions throughout the country with Charley. Often, they are sports or civic events, but sometimes they are for organizations of the blind or for friends of persons who are blind. Charley speaks bluntly at these meetings.

"What happened to me wasn't an unusual change in fortune. Tens of thousands of people lose their vision or the use of arms or legs in accidents—if not in wars—every year. Each of them must find some way to adjust, to meet life's demands. Those demands don't make allowances for the plans to be set aside, the endless wondering about what might have been.

"These lives can be turned into new directions by new interests, as mine was through golf, as golf became *my* way back into the mainstream of life.

"Golf came to me when I desperately needed something to get me interested in living. It worked in my case. But it was merely a *means* that allowed me to use abilities I had. The important thing for any disabled person is to identify those abilities and to find some way, as I found golf, to give a suddenly altered life new and solid meaning.

"Keep working. Keep driving forward. As long as a human being will do that, something of value will be accomplished."

Keep driving forward. If a life can be described in three words, I think those three will be just fine for Charley Boswell.

Don
Klosterman

We call him Gimpy and he laughs. We steal his golf cart and he beats us anyway on legs that, by logic, should never have left a wheelchair. We dance and *he* teaches the new moves.

To those of us who know him well, there was never any question of him dying. Don Klosterman dead, at 27? He would have organized a party for the guardians of the gate, told a few funny stories, had his membership switched to "pending" and been back with us before he was missed.

Klosterman was pretending he was Irish again the day the accident occurred. He was in Canada to play professional football. It was 1957, the offseason and he was skiing down a mountain in Banff to a St. Patrick's Night party he was co-hosting when he rounded a turn and saw a young woman directly in his path. Her left was blocked by a boulder that might, Don thought, cause a broken leg. Ironic. He swerved right to try to slip by her just inside a stand of trees. It was almost dusk, the time when most skiing accidents occur, the light was flat, the trails were beginning to ice up and Klosterman was tired from having been on the slopes much of the day. He didn't make it. He missed the turn and at a speed later estimated at close to 45 miles an hour, hurtled into the trees.

He ricocheted from tree to tree until he fell, unconscious, a rag doll of a human being. His back was torn apart just above the belt line, the spinal cord was severely damaged. He hemorrhaged internally. There were multiple and serious injuries to his head, rib cage, chest and legs.

The small hospital in Banff couldn't handle his needs and he was rushed to a larger one in Calgary, 85 miles away. He received last rites that first night and, again, several operations later, when the incision became badly infected.

He was held in a Stryker frame for five agonizing months. The frame is a weird object that allows a severe-fracture victim to be immobilized and turned over, device and all, to help circulation and to try to prevent debilitating bedsores. On the day he was moved from the Stryker frame to a bed, the neurosurgeon who had performed three of the eight major operations that Klosterman had, told Don he would never walk again.

"The hell you say," Klosterman exploded. "Get out of here; you're fired." Klosterman picked up a vase of flowers from his bedside and hurled them at the doctor, hitting him squarely in the back as he turned to leave. "First time I ever threw behind my receiver," he would joke to me—later. But that night he cried, for the first time since the accident.

"A lot of people have a desire to win," Klosterman's college football coach, Jordan Olivar, once told me, "but they won't do anything about it except wish. Don will do whatever work is necessary to win."

The next morning, Klosterman calmly assessed his liabilities: Spinal cord injury is one of the most catastrophic injuries a human can sustain and still live. The cord is the cable that transmits messages between the brain and the rest of the body. When it is damaged, every body function below the point of injury is affected. The force that whipped Klosterman from tree to tree had caused many of those nerves to be badly pinched and, in some cases, destroyed. He was partially, and permanently, paralyzed from the waist down.

He had no feeling in vast areas below the injury: his buttocks, portions of his thighs, most of his legs below the knees and both feet. He could feel neither the sharp, probing jabs of the physician's pin nor electric shock applied in attempts to force involuntary muscle movement. It was as if a massive and permanent dose of Novocaine had been administered.

There was no movement below his knees. He had no control of his bladder or bowels. His legs, an athlete's legs, resembled those of the concentration camp survivors of World War II. He weighed 130 pounds.

Klosterman's rehabilitation began that morning. When his therapist came in, Don hired her for two additional workouts a day on her own time. It would be another month before Klosterman could get out of bed, so he tried every kind of exercise in bed he could. He would flop onto his stomach and try to raise each leg at the knee, using what muscle strength remained in his thighs. "It was as if someone was holding my feet down," he told me, "and pressed harder every time I tried to lift a leg." He tried "sets" of these, 10 lifts 10 times, rest, then 10 more. He did it daily until he and the bed linen were drenched in sweat.

During Klosterman's junior year in college, his school, Loyola of Los Angeles, was trailing a strong and favored University of San Francisco team. Klosterman called a pass play that would take his end down and out to the left sideline. His receiver ran the wrong pattern and San Francisco's Ollie Matson, who was to become a many-time All-Pro back in the National Football League, intercepted and scored.

Unshaken—he knew the call and the pass had been good —Klosterman picked the same play again as soon as Loyola regained possession. Again, the same receiver missed the proper "cut" and, again, a touchdown for Matson.

Klosterman ran off the field and up to Coach Jordan Olivar and shouted reassuringly, "Don't worry, coach. We'll get them." He then had a talk with his receiver. Back into the game; same call. This time the receiver followed the pattern, beat Matson and scored. Klosterman kept throwing and Loyola won an upset, 42–28.

Still in bed, he was soon working, alone and with the therapist, four hours a day. Progress was interminably slow and he drew on his football training for psychological support.

When you play football, you come to understand that it takes time to learn. You can't measure your progress day by day on the practice field, but you know that if you stay with whatever it is you're trying to learn, you will improve. Klosterman needed that insight as he labored day after day for months to get some movement from the muscles that remained undamaged in his legs and feet.

"I began to live each day for that day alone," he told me. "I stopped agonizing about yesterday or the future. 'Today, I will work,' I said; 'today, I will get a little better.' I couldn't accept a doctor's statement that I would not walk again. It was inconceivable to me that I would be confined to a wheelchair for the rest of my life."

The desire to "win" and the confidence that he would win now became concentrated in the many steps that comprise rehabilitation following spinal cord damage: to sit up in bed; to stand at bedside; to concentrate on forcing movement in the muscles that allow a foot to be raised or lowered. He had no movement in either one. His feet simply hung at the end of each leg, pointing downward, mute testimony to his lack of control.

For three months Klosterman worked silently, talking only with his therapist and his mother, who had come to Calgary to stay near her thirteenth child. There were days when, football insights aside, Klosterman wondered if he knew what he was doing. Had he reached the point of maximum return from his undamaged muscles? Had the fired neurosurgeon been right? Don had lived. He had fooled the doctors twice after they had called for a priest. Perhaps that would be the limit of his victory. To walk, you have to be able to lift your feet. And, after three exhausting months, his still hung, immovable toes still pointing down. But to quit. . . .

In Klosterman's sophomore year, College of the Pacific quarterbacked by Eddie Le Baron, ripped Loyola, 52–0. The following season, COP scored 20 points against Loyola in the first eight minutes of play. Olivar at the sideline was doing some mental arithmetic: "Eight minutes into 60 minutes is about eight; eight times 20 points is 160 to nothing." Klosterman saw Olivar holding his head and bounced over to him, "Plenty of time, coach. Plenty of time." Klosterman then threw three touchdown passes, scored a fourth touchdown himself with 30 seconds left and kicked all five extra points as Loyola won, 35–33. Only an upset by a strong Santa Clara team kept Loyola from an undefeated season and the Orange Bowl that year.

As Klosterman began to repeat the endless exercises one morning, he felt something quiver inside his left foot. He saw nothing, but he felt the tiniest "flick." It was the first movement he had felt in any of his damaged areas since the accident almost six months before.

He told his doctor. The physician was skeptical. Several days later, the "flick" became visible. It was the briefest kind of tendon movement. By itself, it lifted nothing. But it was a start. Klosterman's therapist cried a bit in joy for her "American friend," then looked at him and asked, "Aren't you happy?"

"Not enough," he replied. "Now we have to get the right foot. I can't walk without both."

That small gain convinced Klosterman he was right. If

sheer work could bring some return of function, he would walk because work was within *his* area of control. He was, he noted later, "elated, but I wasn't going to show anybody until I had it all." He returned to the exercises. It was a month and a half before movement began to return to the right foot.

About six months after he entered the hospital, they allowed him to stand. He stood at bedside for just a moment, supported by hospital aides on both sides. "It was as if I had never stood before," he said. "I couldn't move. I was leaning against the bed. People were holding me. But I was eight feet tall."

Soon, into a wheelchair and to the hospital therapy room. Now what Klosterman was to call the "ball game" began. The rest had been the preliminaries. If Klosterman was to prove the neurosurgeon wrong, it would be done here.

So much we take for granted in life: miraculously—because science has yet to understand fully how—a heart pumps, lungs open and close, we walk. Klosterman, holding onto two long bars parallel to the floor—one on each side of him—was to see if he could learn to walk all over again. For that was what he would have to do. He knew he would never walk as others walk. He could not put down heel, ball, toes as the non-handicapped person does. He would not have that much control over his feet. All he had were his thigh muscles and some unimpaired muscle use in his feet.

Klosterman slowly began to put together what famed orthopedist Robert Kerlan was to call "the only high wire act I've seen on the ground."

With Loyola's running attack stopped by a powerful Florida team one Saturday night, harassed himself by Florida's strong defensive line, Klosterman threw 63 passes and completed 33 for 372 yards (all national records; Don was the leading college passer in the nation that year). Many more passes were in his receivers' hands and were dropped. In town for a game the following day with Los Angeles, Cleveland's Paul Brown watched the passing exhibition and made Klosterman a first-round draft choice, not a small compliment coming from what was then the best team in professional football.

Four of the National Football League's outstanding quarterbacks—Otto Graham and George Ratterman in Cleveland and, later, Bob Waterfield and Norm Van Brocklin in Los Angeles where Don was traded—kept Klosterman on the bench.

Cocky, impatient, Klosterman went off to play in Canada. There also he could more easily pursue skiing, a new love.

Over the next two months, holding onto those bars, he slowly began to walk. It wasn't walking as we know it. It was a peculiar style, one "invented" by Klosterman. He had taught himself to "throw" each foot out—toes, ball, heel making contact in that order, just the reverse of the normal step.

He could no longer walk instinctively. With the nerves that had carried messages between his lower legs and brain gone, he had to consciously plan each step. Each step would take intense concentration. It would be so for the rest of his life. To this day, he is acutely conscious of the movements that comprise a step for him. Conversation remains difficult while he is walking because he walks with his mind.

Eight months after the accident, Klosterman was discharged to his Calgary apartment—for little more than a day. A heating pad vibrator, intended to aid blood circulation, was left on too long. Klosterman, who couldn't feel the heat, was burned to the bone. He returned to the hospital, developed a staph infection and was placed in isolation for more than two months. His limited strength totally sapped by the infection, all he could do was lie in bed. His therapy—and his progress—halted.

Finally, 11 months after the accident, Klosterman went back to California to complete his recuperation. He made one final stop before he left the hospital. He visited the office of the neurosurgeon who had predicted life in a wheelchair, threw both crutches in, said, "I told you I would walk," took three or four steps and fell. Klosterman issued another line from the floor: "Furthermore, I'm going to play golf again—*this* season." In California his therapy resumed. He walked with leg and back braces and on crutches. But he walked.

And he got married. He was wearing metal leg braces the night of his bachelor's party, but they didn't keep a couple of marinated guests from throwing him into the pool in the early hours. When they realized what they had done, they went in after him.

They had no chance. Klosterman went under twice, gasping for breath. By the time his friends reached him, he fought them off and clothes, braces, shoes and all, swam a slow full length of the pool, a polite demonstration of one-upmanship, and then climbed out by himself.

He had said he would take his leg braces off for the last time on the morning of his wedding and he did. He walked that day without aid of any sort. It was a long ceremony, a high nuptial Mass, and at its conclusion when Klosterman turned to kiss his bride, he found himself standing on her train. Balance was then—as now—a problem, but slowly he stepped off and escorted his wife back up the long aisle.

Jobless and broke—medical bills had wiped out the money he had—Klosterman began to sell insurance, once again under the direction of his old Loyola coach, Jordan Olivar, an insurance executive during the offseason. He did well. Olivar, who accompanied Klosterman on calls during the training period, was to tell me: "Wherever we went, as soon as the person we were calling on opened his office door, he invariably would boom, 'Don, great to see you. Come on in.' It wasn't pity; many of the people he called on weren't aware of the accident. It was a response to the warmth of this man."

Klosterman was lifting weights during his off-hours at a gym that was also used by a number of the football players from the University of Southern California. One of them, Ron Mix, an All-American offensive tackle, had been the first draft choice of the Baltimore Colts. Klosterman was advising Mix as a friend about the contractual requests he should make. The American Football League was being formed and the Los Angeles Chargers—soon to move to San Diego—also were trying to sign Mix. But they were having no luck. Frank Leahy, the former Notre Dame coach and then general manager of the Chargers, asked Don if he would help recruit players. Mix was the first assignment. Klosterman signed him to a two-year contract in their first meeting, then quickly gathered several more outstanding athletes for a team and a league that was yet to play a game.

Impressed, Leahy hired Klosterman to work for the Chargers full time. He joined a management/coaching group in 1960 that included Al Davis, now chief executive of the Oakland Raiders, and Chuck Noll, coach of the two-time world champion Pittsburgh Steelers.

Barely out of therapy, still in pain, Klosterman had returned to football. The intelligence and leadership ability that had drawn players to him and helped him lead teams on the field now helped him to direct their management. And, always, it was his knowledge of players, his ability to understand them and in turn be understood, liked and trusted, that worked for him. His enticement in signing new players, of course, was money; but it was his open, low-key empathy and friendliness that permitted him to sign the number of high-quality athletes he did sign.

He would have success wherever he went. After two

years with the Chargers—an early force in the AFL aided by such Klosterman-signed players as Mix, quarterbacks Jack Kemp and John Hadl, and running back Keith Lincoln— Klosterman was hired by Lamar Hunt, owner of the Dallas Texans, as director of player personnel. The Texans were one season away from becoming the Kansas City Chiefs. Athletes Klosterman selected helped Kansas City win the AFL title in 1967 and the Super Bowl in 1970.

Three years later, Klosterman became general manager of the Houston Oilers. On his first day with the Oilers, six members of the AFL All-Star team approached him and asked to be traded to Houston. "We want to play for you," they said.

In 1970, Klosterman moved to the Baltimore Colts as general manager. When Colts' owner Carroll Rosenbloom traded his franchise in 1972 for that of the Los Angeles Rams, Klosterman went with him.

Klosterman was a major force in the birth and success of the AFL and its eventual merger with the National Football League. Those were wild years. He found himself part talent scout and part undercover agent from the time he joined the Chargers in 1960 until the merger in 1966.

The new league competed with the NFL in signing the better college athletes. It became practice for each team, sometimes represented by league employees, to get to and hide players until they could be signed.

Klosterman integrated one of Dallas' finest apartment complexes when he hid four players the Texans wanted, including Buck Buchanan, a defensive tackle from Grambling, in the apartment across from his. The superintendent, tipped by an angry tenant, came around prying, but the fact that Lamar Hunt owned the building was useful.

Klosterman's wife, Clare, fed the four breakfast. It took her three hours to fill them up.

"How," she wondered aloud to Klosterman, "do we keep these players a secret? I've just given them 160 pancakes, plus a dozen eggs and a loaf of bread I had to borrow from a neighbor whose husband writes for a Dallas paper." Buchanan, 6'8", 280 pounds, amply repaid the meal; he became a five-time All-Pro tackle.

Klosterman took on the city of Minneapolis when he attempted to sign Bobby Bell, two-time All-American from the University of Minnesota, for the Chiefs.

Flying to Minneapolis, Klosterman met Hubert H. Humphrey, former mayor of that city and then the senior senator from Minnesota, on the plane.

Humphrey inquired what business brought Klosterman to Minneapolis.

"I'm going to sign Bobby Bell."

"You'll never get Bobby," Humphrey responded. "He's so popular here he can probably be mayor of Minneapolis if he wants to. The Vikings have drafted him and they'll sign him."

Klosterman met with Bell in the office of Bell's advisor, a Minneapolis businessman. The trio remained in that office for six consecutive hours. For more than five of those hours, as word got out that Bell and Klosterman were there, phone calls started to pour in. Civic leaders, sportswriters and the mayor called to try to intercede for the Vikings.

"There were several times when I thought, 'Oh, God, I'm going to lose him,' " Klosterman told me. " 'Somebody's going to come in here and offer him more money for the Vikings or his advisor will convince him to stay in Minnesota.' "

When Bell's advisor heard the amount of the Texans' offer, he saw Minnesota losing Bell to Dallas and himself losing a large group of friends.

"Who is going to guarantee all this money you're promising Bobby?" he asked Klosterman in a last-ditch move. "Lamar Hunt," Klosterman replied. When he saw the man wasn't familiar with the name, he asked, "Would you like to talk with him on the telephone?"

Klosterman placed the call and introduced the pair. Turned out Bell's advisor had a plant in Dallas. It was in a building and on a tract of land owned by the ubiquitous Hunt.

When the contract was finally signed, Klosterman left by the back door. He was to have met with another player in Minneapolis, but all he wanted was to get out of town. He drove to the airport and asked for the first flight leaving Minneapolis. In any direction.

Klosterman wanted Otis Taylor, an exceptionally fine end. But the NFL had hidden Taylor with another player in a motel in Houston awaiting the NFL draft. Klosterman staked out a scout to watch the motel. The NFL "baby sitters" moved the athletes and lost the scout.

Klosterman called Taylor's mother. They had become friends during his visits to the Taylor home.

"Where's Otis?" he asked.

"I don't know," Mrs. Taylor replied, "But I'm going to call the police and charge someone with kidnapping."

Klosterman's scout called in from Dallas. The players were now in a motel there. Agents from the older league were in the room and in the adjacent corridors, so Klosterman's man couldn't talk to Taylor.

The NFL moved the two players again, to a motel in Fort Worth. Klosterman's scout followed. At three o'clock in the morning, he got the players out of a bathroom window and flew them to Kansas City. Nobody had slept for 48 hours, but the Chiefs had Taylor.

Klosterman's rapport with players is extraordinary—even with players who got away. Gale Sayers, who was to become one of football's finest running backs, was the only number-one draft pick Klosterman couldn't sign. After Sayers came to terms with Chicago, his mother wrote to Klosterman saying,

'I hope the fact that Gale has signed with the Bears will not destroy our friendship. You've been so helpful to Gale and he loves you like a brother. I'm sorry. I didn't want him to go to Chicago, but Gale felt he had to." Gale and Don remain close friends.

In 1966, the Chiefs drafted Aaron Brown, a fine end from the University of Minnesota, in the first round. Klosterman had visited Brown and his family in Louisiana a number of times and Brown had agreed to sign with Kansas City. Hunt flew down to sign Brown. Brown's mother, however, said "No one is going to sign my son unless Mr. Klosterman is here." The signing had to wait until Klosterman chartered a plane and flew to Louisiana.

Klosterman didn't expect to get All-American John Hadl for the Chargers.. After Hadl signed with Klosterman, he said, "You know, there never was any question that I wasn't going to sign with you and San Diego."

"Why?" Klosterman asked.

"Do you remember when Loyola played Kansas and an 11-year-old kid stopped you after the game and asked a hundred questions about throwing a football? You hadn't showered, but you spent a half hour talking about playing quarterback and the importance of hard work?"

"No, I don't remember," Klosterman replied.

"I was the kid," Hadl said. "And I was going to sign with any team you were associated with."

Klosterman's attempt to get San Francisco's John Brodie, the NFL's top passer, to leave the 49ers for a $750,000 contract, helped precipitate the 1966 merger of the two leagues. The New York Giants earlier had signed kicker Pete Gogolak from the AFL's Buffalo Bills. The AFL decided to retaliate and go after key talent, the NFL's quarterbacks. Klosterman made the bid to Brodie on behalf of his league. The size of the prospective contract forced the NFL to realize the high cost of maintaining rival leagues. The merger, which of course was what the AFL wanted, followed. (Brodie never played in the AFL because the raiding ended but his threat of a suit against the two leagues for preventing him from accepting the overture brought him a reported settlement of $921,000 plus lawyers' fees. Whereupon Brodie called Klosterman. His message: "Thanks a million.")

Klosterman kept his promise to play golf again. It was in May 1958, five months after he left the hospital. He had to be set up by his partner for each shot that first round and he fell a half dozen times after swinging, but he played the full 18 holes and scored 93. It was 18 months before he stopped falling and two years before he could swing without someone holding onto the back of his belt.

Because he has, in effect, no lower left leg, he can't turn his stroke into his left side, as right-handed players do. He has learned to turn his left foot out, which allows him to use the strength and balance of his left thigh muscles. A scratch golfer before his accident, Klosterman now shoots consistently between 76 and 85 from the back tees. His handicap is 13, one most golfers would like to have.

Don and I played not too long after he had returned to golf. On the fourth hole, Don hit into a trap. It was a downhill lie. I told him to forget the shot, but he climbed in, hit a fine recovery to the green and fell on his face. He wouldn't let anyone help him up and climbed out alone.

In a foursome later with two of my former New York teammates, Alex Webster and Harland Svare, and myself, Klosterman began to beat us so badly that we stole his golf cart and made him walk. He still won.

When the Baltimore for Los Angeles franchise exchange was approved by the NFL, Rosenbloom and Klosterman left Tampa, Florida, en route to Los Angeles late in the day. They had to make a connection at Atlanta. Rosenbloom was traveling with just a briefcase into which he had stuffed toilet articles and a change of linen. Klosterman, who has a passion for the most horribly colored sports clothes I've ever seen (and many of them), checked four huge suitcases, but insisted on keeping two large carry-on hanging bags. He wouldn't let them go with the luggage or even allow a porter to carry them to the plane in Miami. Don couldn't walk and carry luggage, so his boss ended up carrying Klosterman's bags, which was what Don had in mind all along.

Rosenbloom called ahead for a porter and a wheelchair to meet the plane in Atlanta. He told Klosterman to get into the wheelchair and put the clothes across his lap. "I can't, Carroll," Klosterman said. "I promised myself I would never get into one of those things again."

"If you won't ride, I will," Rosenbloom replied. He sat down and put Klosterman's suits on his lap. The redcap pushed and Don walked alongside, holding onto the arm of the chair.

An elderly couple approached them in the terminal. The man stopped Rosenbloom. "How badly you must be hurt," he said, "if you're riding and *this man* is walking. May I help?" He placed a dollar bill in the lap of one of football's wealthiest men.

Little stops Klosterman. As soon as he became reacquainted with golf, he tried tennis. He gave that up only because "I would embarrass anyone I was playing with." When I said that he was ducking out on my chance to get even for my golf losses, he laughed and said, "I beat you at golf, my friend, and I can beat you at tennis." Maybe he could, at that.

Klosterman, as a kid, was known as rather feisty. The end of his nose was rarely without a wound of some variety. No one goes too far with the older Klosterman either. While he was driving along a street one afternoon with his wife, a young man kept cutting in front of them dangerously close. After it became clear that he was doing it intentionally, Don pulled in front and forced him off the road.

He wobbled back to the other car, reached through the open window and grabbed the driver by his collar.

"I'm going to teach you a lesson now, at your age. You don't do this kind of thing. What if you had tried that with someone who was sick?"

The other driver, bigger than Don, was strangely mute. Just then a car pulled over across the street. The man driving got out and shouted to Don, "Leave that guy alone or I'll show you a thing or two."

"Come on over, my friend," Klosterman replied. "I'll give you a piece of the action."

The man hopped back into his car and drove off.

The pain is still there today. Klosterman's internal damage will never be completely healed. Fatigue pulls at his face when he has to walk more than a block. With the little true muscle support he has, balance remains precarious. Because of the loss of feeling, he doesn't know if his feet are on the ground and how firmly they are planted unless he looks. He has to endure the stares and stupid comments of strangers who taunt "drunk," or ask questions when they see Klosterman's peculiar gait.

Dr. Kerlan calls Klosterman's walking a "minor miracle" because he can't fully explain it. Klosterman's brother, Bob, attributes it to an "extraordinary reserve of strength." Jordan Olivar talks of Klosterman's willingness to pay any price to win.

Explain it? I played in only one football game with Don, the collegiate All-Star East-West game in 1952. We were in the closing seconds, trailing, near midfield with time left for one play. The spectators were leaving and most of us on the

West team were resigned. Klosterman was still fighting. The field and the ball were too wet and muddy to permit passing. So Klosterman called a pass. He sent his split end deep on a straight run and threw a long, perfect pass that hit his receiver in the end zone for the potential winning score—and went through his fingers.

I think of Klosterman today—the best general manager in football and one who last year turned down a million-dollar offer to head the management of the new pro football franchise in Tampa. I think of him playing better golf than I can, out-dancing me, out-talking me, never complaining—and I don't concern myself with questions.

By what do we judge a man? If we measure him by what he does when every sense cries out that he cannot succeed, we will have a fairly good idea of who Don Klosterman is. "Life only demands from you the strength you have," Dag Hammarskjöld wrote. "Only one feat is possible—not to have run away."

This tough, competitive, fun-loving man never ran away from anything in his life.

Floyd
Layne

It was, somehow, a little bit of sun the day they announced the news. Floyd Layne was being hired as varsity basketball coach at City College of New York. Twenty-five years ago, he had been thrown out of CCNY because he had taken money from gamblers to help rig his school's basketball games. It had been stupid—and illegal. But he was young and because he was essentially level-headed, he didn't think his life was over. Punishments fit the crime, don't they?

No, they don't, not always. He was to learn that. Layne went into the army. He played part of a season with the Harlem Globetrotters, returned to college and graduate school.

Then he tried for two decades to find a place for himself in organized sports.

He thought it reasonable that any punishment would in time end. He played basketball in the Eastern League, then a loose organization at the fringe of professional basketball, and attempted to get a tryout in the National Basketball Association. But he found no relaxation of the lifetime ban the NBA had imposed on players involved in game fixing. Eight years in the Eastern League ended with Layne on the outside. Was he forced out? How does one go about proving a feeling in your gut? "When I first played there, the league was independent. Then it wanted to develop an association with the NBA. I heard they couldn't get together until all of us were gone." A fine outfielder, Layne also attempted to enter professional baseball. A contract to play in one of the highest rungs of the minor leagues was offered and then mysteriously withdrawn.

Layne had taken his knowledge of basketball and the black inner city back to one of New York's worst ghettos in 1956. He became director of an after-school recreation center, helping street kids. He worked with youngsters for 15 years. He also helped uncounted college and professional basketball players as coach or personal advisor. The biggest of these names—NBA All-Star Nate Archibald of the Kansas City-Omaha Kings, whom Layne had discovered in his center when Archibald was 12.

Frustrated as an athlete, Layne sought coaching jobs—without success. He did coach a junior college team for two seasons. But when his predecessor asked for his old job back, Layne was released. He kept looking. Often, his applications were ignored, his requests for interviews unanswered. Even though he had coached high school boys at his recreation center for over 10 years at one point, an Ivy League college was to turn him away because, they said, he "lacked sufficient continuous experience on the high-school level."

Finally, after almost two decades, Layne answered a newspaper advertisement in 1974 and was named head coach at CCNY, the place he had once shamed.

Layne, now 47, sat with me recently in his New York bachelor apartment and talked about the last 25 years of his life. "I can tell you about every minute of it," he said softly. Layne is tall—6'3"—and lean. It's a basketball player's body. Alone of all the CCNY men arrested, he is still in the game.

"It's ironic," he told me. "I never met a gambler, never used the money for myself, and never shaved points." During his second year at CCNY Layne was approached by several play-

ers. They had to try hard to get him to agree to do what
athletes on other teams were already doing. District Attorney
Frank S. Hogan told one writer, "Layne was first approached
in the fall . . . but did not agree to go along until December."
Floyd bought his mother a washing machine out of the $3,000
given him, rolled the rest in a handkerchief and buried it in
a flower pot. In return, he was asked to shave points in three
games. But when the time came, "I didn't know how to do it.
I couldn't change the way I played."

Layne shook his head. "Why did I take the money? I still
don't know. To 'go along'? I didn't need the money. We were
poor, but we had enough." Layne was to tell one writer some
years after the scandal, "The kids I worked with at the center
watched me play. They wanted to know why I wasn't in pro
ball. I told them and they asked, 'Why did they keep you out
forever? Why didn't you get a chance?' I couldn't make them
understand."

Layne has no idea of the number of jobs he lost because
he took gamblers' money. "I've long since stopped counting."
He thought of quitting often, of leaving basketball—but the
game is his life.

An intelligent and articulate man, Layne didn't attempt to
minimize what he did. "I made a mistake and I paid a heavy
price for it. But that mistake put my feet on the ground. It
taught me about adversity. It led me to dedicate myself to
kids so they wouldn't make the same kind of error and pay the
same price."

There was a knock on his door and a tall young man entered the room, smiling warmly at Layne. "Thought I'd drop
in, coach," he said, "just to say hello. How you doing?"

Layne greeted his visitor with a bear hug and then introduced Larry to me. He was, I learned after he left, one of
the thousands of boys who had lived in a huge low-income
housing project in New York City's South Bronx. He was a

good basketball and softball player, active in sports in school and in Layne's recreation center. In high school, Larry became involved in a gang fight and one of the boys in the other gang was killed. Larry and several others involved were arrested, charged with manslaughter and sentenced to three-year prison terms.

Layne agonized about Larry, whom he had met in his center six years earlier and had coached. He wondered if he could have kept Larry from the madness of gang fighting. He promised himself that he would try to learn what was going on with the kids in his center who never directly asked for help or who were not brought in by parents or counselors or neighbors—the kind of kids who can quietly or violently slip down the drain before anyone is aware of a problem.

When Larry came up for his parole hearing, Layne asked he be released. He told the parole board that he didn't think Larry would get into trouble again. Larry was paroled. Layne helped him find a job in an accounting office. Floyd had earlier convinced the owner to take a chance. When Larry had settled into his job, Layne urged him to finish high school. Larry did. And then he began college, nights.

All during this time, Larry frequently came to the center to talk with Layne. By the time he was 21, he was a different person—mature, confident of his future. He's married now, with two children, has become a certified public accountant himself and is following the "game plan" he and Layne had laid out together.

"I couldn't prevent Larry from getting into trouble when I first knew him," Layne told me, "but I'd like to think I helped him grow into a good man."

I had known of Floyd's outstanding work with kids and teen-agers. His center was in a tough neighborhood. Most of the youngsters living there were good kids, but in that environment many them became the so-called unreachables.

Layne didn't wait for them to come to him. He went out looking. He went into courts and homes, counseled on street cor-
ners, talked with school guidance counselors, wherever and
whenever he thought he could help someone.

He sought out the truants, those who had already dropped
out of school, the ones with budding delinquency records. If
he heard of an impending gang fight, he wouldn't let gang
members out of the center, literally locking the doors. He was
tuned in to the grapevine and frequently prevented street
problems by getting to leaders before things happened. In his
quiet voice, he reached them and they listened to him.

The South Bronx was—and is—dying. The anguish of that
part of New York City misses few. A black mother walks her
three children to and from school every day for fear they will
otherwise meet a drug addict. Mrs. Perez sends her honor-
student son off to fifth grade in the morning and finds him, at
lunchtime, dead in an abandoned car behind her home.

A doctor experienced in a South Bronx emergency ward
wrote a medical paper and referred almost parenthetically to
"one of the bloodiest civilian battlefields of the northeast."
The paper dealt with expedient methods of caring for knife
wounds of the chest and abdomen. Few police precincts in
New York exceed those of the South Bronx in crime.

Layne, a modest man, says merely that he tried "to be a
positive influence, a good example." He prodded kids: How
are your grades? Who are you hanging around with? When
are you returning to school; there's no action for you unless
you finish.

Many listened. Many did not. One of his members was
knifed to death just outside the center doors in a fight over
drugs. Another was shot and killed during an attempted rob-
bery of a subway cashier. Layne worked hard. "Sometimes,"
he told me, "I had to throw a youngster into a wall to get his
attention."

So many identified with Layne. Proudly. "I belong to Mr. Layne's center." Or, "I play ball for Mr. Layne's team." They wanted to please him. A teen-ager who saw no usefulness in school would stay because "Mr. Layne" thought it was important. To many, Layne was parent as well as coach.

I asked Floyd how many victories there were. "We won a lot, but we lost some, too. So many we couldn't save. The boy knifed outside the center. He was a good boy."

His recreation center, like others established in crowded ghetto areas throughout New York, was sometimes a life-saving operation, geared to help youngsters stay out of trouble. It was a place where boys and girls could come to develop skills, make friends, participate in sports, have a chance to talk with someone when they faltered.

Parents sought Layne's help. A distraught mother asked him to speak with her teen-age daughter who was becoming deeply involved with a much older man. The girl was coming in late at night, disregarding curfews set by her parents, and was ready to drop out of school. She wouldn't heed her parents' warnings and they were desperate.

Floyd succeeded in counseling this young girl where her parents had been unable to. He got her back into the stream of social activities with teen-agers. He encouraged her in her schoolwork and supported her growing interest in nursing. He got to her in time. Today, she says candidly that if it hadn't been for Layne's intervention at a critical moment, she wouldn't be the registered nurse she is now, enjoying both a career and a happy family.

Mike and David, twin brothers, were 16 and in trouble all the time when Layne met them. They stole cars, shoplifted, missed more school than they attended. When they did go to classes, they disrupted them to the point where they were thrown out of school. Both of them were headed for serious problems, behavior that in their neighborhood could easily have escalated to felonies.

Layne discovered their interest in basketball. He brought them into his center and put them on one of his teams. He coached them and watched them. The center became "their home."

Floyd used basketball to channel their combative spirits, and set an example they could understand. They no longer had to drink to "feel good." They could get their highs from being the leading scorers in a tightly contested basketball game. Layne was able to crack their shells and reach for strengths within each of them. He redirected them toward attainable goals and they, too, were helped because a basketball coach cared enough—and tried hard enough.

Layne has helped an estimated 400 boys and girls reach—and finish—college. He held out its benefits to teen-agers who had never considered college. He talked to high school teachers and advisors. He spoke with college administrators. For those who had sports talent, he spoke to coaches. He found scholarships. He saw that money was available for clothes, for transportation.

Archibald was an example. He had become one of "Mr. Layne's boys" while he was still in junior high school. He soaked up all the basketball he could get. Layne was to call him "the soundest player in the fundamentals of the game I ever coached." When Archibald reached high school, he wasn't on the team during his sophomore year. Layne met with the coach. Archibald played during his junior and senior years and went on to college.

"Floyd was a tremendous influence in my life," Archibald was to say. "He was responsible for keeping me off the streets. He told me I had the ability to finish high school and college. He encouraged me. He made me pursue a career in basketball. "There isn't enough I can say about what he did for me."

Twenty-five years ago, college basketball was far more important than the professional game. The National Basketball

Association had only recently been formed. There were franchises in places like Moline, Fort Wayne, Sheboygan and Waterloo. The New York Knicks played most of their home games in an armory. The first black player was about to be drafted, Chuck Cooper of Duquesne.

Madison Square Garden was the mecca of the college basketball world. Spectators flocked there to see college teams from Kentucky, Bradley, Utah, St. John's, Long Island University. It was there that CCNY became known as the Cinderella team.

Twenty-five years ago, only one sport mattered to CCNY students and fans. That was basketball. The school's football and baseball teams were undistinguished. But basketball teams in 31 years under Coach Nat Holman had won 383 games and lost only 132.

And none of those teams was as good as the '50–'51 club.

With four sophomores on the starting five, CCNY became the only school—to this day—to win both the season-culminating National Invitation Tournament and the National Collegiate Athletic Association tournament in the same year.

Floyd Layne, Ed Roman, Ed Warner and Al Roth all were New York City residents who had turned aside the blandishments of colleges throughout the country to play for Holman. Each had been an all-city high school athlete. When they became eligible for the varsity as sophomores, they pushed everyone except senior Irv Dambrot to the sidelines. Even cocaptain Joe Galiper was benched.

Layne, whom Holman had changed from a forward to a guard, became the defensive star. He always drew the assignment of stopping an opponent's high scorer.

CCNY was the last team invited to both the NIT and NCAA tourneys. Both times, they were unseeded.

City's first game in the NIT was against the defending champion, San Francisco. The West Coast team was heavily favored to win in a rout. But it never happened.

Holman abandoned his fast break offense, matched his opponents' slower, more deliberate style and beat them at their own game. Warner drove through San Francisco almost at will to score 26 points as CCNY won easily, 65–46.

Kentucky, next, received the worst beating in its history, 89–50. (A Kentucky state senator would rise in the legislature the following day and ask that the state flag be lowered to half-mast in mourning.) The school that had been number one in the nation in 1948, 1949, and 1950, didn't know what to do with a team it hadn't respected enough even to scout. Holman started substitute Leroy Wadkins, 6'8", to jump center for the opening ball against Kentucky's seven-footer, Bill Spivey. Wadkins got the tap and then Roman, two inches shorter, came in. He was to score 17 that night behind Warner's second consecutive 26 and Dambrot's 20.

"We were sky-high for that game," Layne was to recall with me, "and we didn't come down until the game was over."

In the opening minutes, Roman, who had a fine hook shot with either hand, spun to his right to shoot and Spivey reached over and slammed the ball into the stands. On the next sequence of plays, Roman got it again, this time faked right and spun left. Again Spivey and again into the spectators' laps.

Holman immediately switched Roman and Warner. Roman went to the corner, drawing Spivey out with him, and put in four quick one-handers against the seven-footer who was somewhat lost at defending a forward. Warner, as versatile an athlete as Roman, finished at center.

Duquesne fell by 10 and then it was Bradley, the number-one team in the nation that season with two All-Americans, Paul Unruh and 5'8½" Gene Melchiorre.

By then, CCNY had been well-scouted. Layne had to stop Melchiorre. He did. The Bradley star, who frequently scored 25 points a game, was held to 16.

Bradley led at the half. The lead changed seven times in

the next 15 minutes. Trailing by one point with five minutes left, CCNY broke away to win by eight.

Warner, who had scored 87 points in four games, was elected the Most Valuable Player in the tournament. Holman's sophomores had given him and CCNY their first invitation championship.

The four consecutive upsets had captivated a basketball-conscious country. In spite of its NIT victory, City again was the last team invited to the NCAA tournament. Again, the school was the underdog in every game it would play. The experts may have believed that, but basketball fans were beginning to realize this was a special team.

In the first game, Ohio State went into a tight zone defense that successfully choked off Roman and Warner. Layne, the only starter still using the two-handed set shot, took their place. Shooting from 20 to 25 feet out, he scored 17 points as City squeaked through, 56–55. North Carolina State lost and then it was the finals and Bradley again.

With less than two minutes remaining, CCNY led by eight. The New York crowd, savoring a second tournament victory, had been on its feet since the fourth quarter began. Bradley substituted two faster players for taller ones and began to press on defense. The Illinois team scored seven consecutive points in 60 seconds, five of them by Melchiorre. One point separated the clubs. The partisan crowd was screaming.

Melchiorre stole the ball again and drove in for what would have been the winning basket. As he went up, the ball flew loose. Dambrot grabbed it, threw it upcourt to substitute Norm Mager who was unguarded and Mager scored. 71–68.

CCNY in 18 days had accomplished what no other team had ever done.

CCNY's sweep held page one for days as even marginal sports fans paused a moment to enjoy the success of a team that wasn't supposed to win. Mayor William O'Dwyer of New

York toasted the team. *Life* magazine devoted two pages to a huge picture. *Sports* gave it a cover.

"This is," said the Garden's promoter, Ned Irish, "potentially one of the great college teams of all time."

Ten months later, the entire first team was in court and *Life* gave five pages "to the greatest scandal since the Chicago Black Sox tried to dump the World Series."

Junius Kellogg, a center on Manhattan's team, ended the game rigging. Approached by a fixer, Kellogg pretended agreement but told District Attorney Hogan. Within days, 15 players were arrested and confessed. Eventually seven schools and 32 players including 10 All-Americans and the heart of the gold medal winning 1948 U.S. Olympic basketball team became involved.

But no school was hit as hard—or seemed to inflict as much public pain—as the one basketball fans had adopted in '50–'51 as its own. It was as if Frank Merriwell and Jack Armstrong had been caught in the Brinks job.

Holman, one of the legends of basketball, was suspended for "conduct unbecoming a teacher." The conduct was never specified by the college and Holman won reinstatement two years later after he took the matter to court. CCNY de-emphasized basketball and left Madison Square Garden to play in its school gymnasium. It has yet to come out.

Kentucky, a club its coach Adolph Rupp had said "gamblers couldn't touch with a 10-foot pole," had been reached instead by a mere $500, the price several of his players had taken to fix a game.

LIU was on its way to number-one ranking in the country. It, too, retreated to its college gym.

Kentucky's Rupp tried to make a case for some of the players: "The Chicago Black Sox threw games," he said, "but these kids only shaved points." Many were puzzled by the distinction. ("Shaving points" means controlling the final point differential in a ball game. A bookmaker explains: "UCLA is playing a weak team. No one would bet against UCLA in a straight win-lose proposition. So bookmakers stir action by giving the weaker team a number of points, say, 20. If UCLA wins by 21 or more, the UCLA betters win.")

Some players drew short jail terms. Most, including Layne, received suspended sentences.

The scandal that ensnared the athletes was primarily the product of school administrators and coaches far older, more mature, and more devious than the players. The administrators put up, or countenanced the putting up by "friends," of huge amounts of money to recruit and keep athletes happy. ("Don't they realize," asked writer Red Smith, "that a boy who can be taught to take money for shooting baskets can also be taught to take money for missing them?")

The charges against the 32 were varied, but they were primarily for intentionally losing games their teams were supposed to win and/or seeing that their teams won or lost by fewer points than they were supposed to. In both cases, gamblers on the inside could win huge sums.

But the players alone were punished by the law. The coaches and the school policy makers for the most part continued their old if temporarily diminished practices. The *indirect* punishment meted out to the players was excessive.

"The American people have a romanticized view of athletics," Layne's teammate Ed Roman, now a school psychologist in New York, was later to say. "They want to identify with the fantasy that the world of sports has come to represent. Whenever you break a moral code that people think they are supposed to believe in, you're confronted with a wrath that's much stronger than any burglar or common thief ever faces."

Layne is back at CCNY now, but he had returned to society a long time ago. His ability to understand what he had done at the age of twenty—and to realize he could recover and, more, perhaps help others avoid the same kind of mistake—had long "repaid" the misstep of 25 years ago. The man whose tip touched off the scandal revelations, Junius Kellogg of Manhattan College, was the first to acknowledge it. Kellogg had become a youth worker for New York City after college.

"Floyd has salvaged at least a thousand kids I know of," Kellogg said. "No overstatement can be made of his work. He's done more for society than most of us."

At Layne's first game as CCNY coach, he was welcomed by a number of young men he had helped while working in the shadow of sports. There was a boy there too, a guest of Layne's, on leave from a state training school. "He's just a kid who was in school," he told me, "and had a fight with someone else. The other boy fell, hit his head and died. It's something that could have happened to anyone in the South Bronx, but most people, the ones who have relatively clean lives, don't understand that."

When Layne was named CCNY's basketball coach, he said simply, "I've traveled a wide circle to get back home. I've never asked for any sympathy or any handouts. All I want is a chance."

And that's why I said a little sunshine appeared the day CCNY said it would hire Layne. They decided he had served "his time" and since he was qualified, he could have the job. Prosecution for a crime, someone there realized, doesn't mean persecution.

Charlie
Conerly

The first time I saw Charlie Conerly, I thought, *My God, what an old son of a bitch to be playing football.* His prematurely gray hair jutted out below a beaten baseball cap. His socks were falling down. He had on a semblance of a football uniform. No pads because he didn't plan on getting into contact.

It was August 1952. I'd just come from the University of Southern California where all the players hollered and cheered and ran a thousand yards on every practice play. Charlie never took a step he didn't have to. He never said a word he didn't have to. His face seemed to have just one expression: the leading edge of slumber.

Four years before, he had been the National Football League's unanimous choice for Rookie of the Year. His passing with a team that was to win only four games surpassed the first-year records of Sammy Baugh and Bob Waterfield, still playing then but already legends.

The year before that, Charlie had been on virtually every All-American team in the country at the University of Mississippi.

Now, in 1952, he was quarterback of a Giant team that was coming apart. The Giants would lose 14 games over the next two seasons.

Hampered by a coach, Steve Owen, whose primary concern

was defense, by ends who had little speed and couldn't hold onto passes, and by a porous line that gave him virtually no protection, Charlie was taking an extraordinary physical beating from opposing linemen.

In one game in 1953, Charlie threw four touchdown passes to upset a far superior Philadelphia team and knock it out of contention for the conference title. On 12 consecutive plays in that game, Philadelphia end Norm Willey slammed into Charlie just after he had released the ball. Willey weighed about 225, Charlie 190. Charlie didn't say a word to the tackle who was supposed to be blocking Willey. But he kept calling pass plays knowing that Willey would undoubtedly be coming through again.

It's easy for a quarterback to know who missed his block. Just catch the number of the truck and you know where it comes from. But Charlie would never get on a Giant lineman. "They're doing their best," he'd say. "You can't ask more of a man than that." Yet—and this rarely happens in football—I can recall a number of our linemen apologizing to Charlie. Several even muttered regrets to Charlie's wife, Perian.

"I'm just not big enough," an offensive guard once told Perian. "I can't keep them off Charlie. Just once I wish he'd give me a little hell in the huddle. I'd feel better."

Hell in the huddle. A Detroit tackle once remembered how quarterback Bobby Layne reacted when line play wasn't up to his standard. "If you ever missed a block, Layne made sure everybody knew about it, guys on the field, guys on the bench, everybody in the stadium knew it. Layne would . . . call you right out of the huddle. He'd stand there, raving at you and shaking a finger in your face . . . ." But this just wasn't Charlie's way.

Charlie was a mass of cuts, tears and welts from September through December. He was a truly battered man. "He's taken more beatings than anybody I've ever seen," our team doctor once told me.

The Giant offense was choked to death in 1953. Teams used seven or eight men rushing on the line, scornful comment on the ability of our ends. So we had great trouble running. The leading pass receivers that year were two backs, Kyle Rote and Eddie Price.

As the Giants floundered, the fans got angry—as only New York fans can. Because the quarterback was the man with the ball, he was the center of all eyes. Charlie would throw a pass that looked bad and they'd scream at him. What they didn't know was that Charlie often grounded the ball rather than take the loss. It's illegal, but through necessity, Charlie became a master at grounding the ball.

He also became the most abused athlete I've ever seen. One would have to be the focal point of the boos and jeers of thousands to appreciate the anguish and frustration Charlie knew. Signs bloomed throughout the Polo Grounds with variations on the theme: "Conerly, go home." Spectators waited for him to leave so they could insult him at close range. When a group of us attended a hockey game in Madison Square Garden with our families that year and were introduced, the entire crowd jeered. As always, Charlie took the brunt of it. A man spotted him and started cursing him.

Some of the coaches tried to explain things. "When you see that thundering herd charging you," end coach Jim Lee Howell told some writers, "and you know you're going to be blasted, it takes guts to stand there and not panic. Charlie has that courage and a lot of other things the public doesn't appreciate. He's been our meal ticket for 10 years. We don't send in more than one play in 10 from the bench. That means he not only takes that pounding, but he gets up and calls those plays and runs that team."

To little avail. Some years the abuse was so bad Perian and Charlie just wouldn't go out evenings. He'd be recognized and he didn't want Perian embarrassed.

Even our wives were fair game for critics of the team and

Charlie's in particular. One afternoon when spectators were screaming, "Get Conerly out of there, send in Heinrich" (Don Heinrich, the number-two quarterback), one woman began to shriek at the wives seated nearby: "Your husbands stank today, especially that bum Conerly. Why didn't they play Heinrich? Eat the ball, eat the ball. That's all that dumb coward Conerly knows how to do." And on and on.

Charlie's wife, Perian, ignored her, but the wife next to Perian finally had it. She whipped around, almost nose to nose with the other woman. "It's obvious you don't know anything about football or you'd know it takes guts to eat the ball and be plowed under by two or three big linemen. It takes skill to deliberately throw the ball away when your receivers are covered. And if Charlie had a line in front of him today, he wouldn't have had to do either." All of this delivered flat out with malice—and fury—aforethought.

"Ahhh, you must be Mrs. Conerly," the woman jeered.

"No, I'm not, I'm Mrs. Heinrich."

One "fan" was momentarily silenced.

During one game during that disastrous '53 season, Charlie completed nine consecutive passes in the first quarter. The tenth fell incomplete—and the boos began. Charlie and Perian and my wife, Maxine, and I went out to dinner one night. Two men who had obviously lost money on our four-point victory over Washington the previous week came to our table and accused Charlie of purposely not scoring from the one-yard line so the Giants would not exceed the four and one-half point spread we had been favored by. I asked them if the Giants had "tricked up the movies that showed Charlie scoring twice without the officials calling it." They disappeared.

Sportswriters stoked much of the discontent. (One "blessing" of those early bad years: there was no national coverage of pro football. We would all go home after being gone from

August through December and friends would ask, "Where've you been?" Pro football for years to come would play to empty seats; its coverage then was relegated to the back pages of sports sections.) In New York virtually every time the Giants lost, headlines rose the following day: "When will the Giants replace Conerly?" "Conerly too old; must go." He was then 32.

There were exceptions, of course. One columnist noted late in 1953: "The fans take delight in voicing their disapproval of Conerly whenever he is trapped behind the line of scrimmage while attempting to pass. They feel he takes too much time finding his targets and therefore is forced to eat the ball much too often. Those who criticize Conerly for taking too much time . . . should look downfield sometimes and see what's happening. Potential receivers are so well covered by defensive players that it would be suicide to throw the ball. . . ."

After a 14–10 New York loss to Pittsburgh in November 1953, Scripps-Howard columnist Joe King wrote, "Conerly was dazzling with his passing although he completed only 17 of 36. . . . If he had even one of a dozen quality ends in the league, he could have had three or four touchdowns with his passing. Giant backs . . . made an effort to win without help from a wretched offensive line that often blocked itself and its runners, but seldom the Steelers."

During this time, most winning teams had at least one receiver, sometimes two, who had the speed and the hands to break a game wide open, among them Pete Pihos, Tom Fears, Elroy "Crazylegs" Hirsch, Billy Wilson, Cloyce Box, Bill Howton and Bobby Walston. Bill Swiacki, who retired in 1949, was the only end Charlie ever had to finish among the league's ten top receivers. His main targets became backs Kyle Rote and me, neither of us known for blazing speed.

". . . The way our guards and ends are playing," wisecracked Giant scout Jack Lavelle, "maybe they help write the anti-Conerly signs."

My admiration for Charlie grew as he took this physical and verbal abuse silently, without responding, without showing anger, without making excuses to the writers when they came to him for postgame questions. He had a built-in excuse; in 1952 and 1953, we were a bunch of humpty dumpties. There was a reserve, a pride about Charlie that would not allow explanations, however legitimate, let alone alibis. Even in the good year of 1957, Charlie played most of the season with a shoulder separation, not telling anyone because the Giants had no other quarterback, not saying anything when sportswriters wondered in print why his throwing accuracy suffered.

The rest of us were not as well controlled as he. After one game near the end of the 1953 season, a bunch of hecklers waited close to two hours until we had changed and left the Polo Grounds. As Charlie walked out, one of them started on him. Charlie kept walking. I was a few steps behind. The guy turned to me and kept talking about "your goddamned quarterback." I was so frustrated that I hit him. I'd never done anything like that before or since. But to see this idiot waiting so long to insult someone who had already taken an unbelievable pounding on the field that day was more than I could handle.

An articulate man when he was with close friends—and felt like talking—it was difficult for Charlie even to talk routinely about himself. He was in the worst of the fighting on Guam as a marine during World War II; his unit went in on the third wave. But he would never discuss it even in later years when we were roommates and the closest of friends. Writer Bill Heinz, assigned by *Life* several years later to do a cover story on Charlie, made a date to have dinner and talk. Charlie asked me to join them. I kept my mouth shut during the early part of the interview; unfortunately so did Charlie. I saw the story vanishing.

Good writers probe for visceral feelings. So Bill would ask, "How do you feel when you get four or five mammoth linemen bearing down on you?"

"Hell, I just throw the ball away," Charlie would respond.

"Well, how do you feel about taking this beating for so many years?"

"I just give him the ball (gesturing to me) and he gets hit."

How to become famous, by Charlie Conerly.

The story was saved, however, because as Charlie concentrated on his steak, Bill Heinz and I concentrated on Charlie.

Perian usually tried to lurk in the background when interviewers called, "eager," she said, "to compensate for Charlie's unfortunate character traits. I know that when the reporter asks, 'Have you ever played any sports besides football?', Charlie will say 'No.' Since reticence has never been one of my strong points, I quickly interject 'Oh, come now . . .' and bombard the writer with a documentation of Charlie's prowess: Charlie hit .467 as an outfielder his senior year at Ole Miss and received several attractive offers to enter professional baseball. For good measure, I throw in that Charlie set three national passing records in 1947 and 26 school records, most of which stood until Archie Manning, now of the New Orleans Saints, broke them in 1969."

When I visited Charlie during the research for this book, I told my old roommate that Perian had better be in the house when I got there. She was—and I talked with Charlie, one of my dearest friends, largely through his "interpreter." "Charlie, do you remember that game in 1954 when . . .?" Perian gave Charlie 10 seconds to ask about my golf, then swiftly, precisely delivered the answer. (Perian wrote an excellent nationally syndicated "backstage with a football team" column during Charlie's 14 years with the Giants. When she was casting about for a name for a collection of her columns in book form, "a friend who had a flair for salesmanship" suggested: *My Fourteen Years as a Pro*. Charlie, who treasured Perian's amateur standing, dismissed that title.)

Charlie was a superb all-around athlete—one of the reasons he could take the pounding and play so consistently well until he was 40. Like many natural athletes, he made everything look deceptively easy, almost casual. However, spectators want more for their money. They want to see Willie Mays charging in from centerfield, cap flying off, or Arnie Palmer pulling up his pants and talking to himself when he's four strokes down with three holes to go. Charlie was never terribly impressed when he succeeded in a play or a game. That's what he was expected to do. You could never tell by looking at his face if he had thrown a 60-yard touchdown pass or if the ball had been intercepted.

I played with two quarterbacks, Charlie and Y.A. Tittle. In the huddle during a tight game, Y.A. gained the confidence of his team with his effervescence and enthusiasm: "Okay, this is it now. I need time to get it off. Now come on, chief, pick up that dog. He's been getting to me. If we blow this one, we've blown the whole damn thing. Okay, now, dammit, keep 'em out of here. Flanker right, IX right, L zig in." It was excitement and it commanded attention.

Charlie obtained the same respect and the same effort in a different manner: "I'll need a little more time on this. Flanker right. L zig in. And I guess we'd better run a IX on the right." It came out slowly and deliberately and there was no doubt in our minds that it would work.

Charlie's decision to retire in 1953, his return, and his relationship with Vince Lombardi fascinated me. Although Charlie never said anything about New York's poor talent or coaching, beneath his passive exterior, he obviously was hurt in 1953. He was—is—a sensitive, introspective man. He was also a perfectionist although he would have denied it. He hated to lose; he had never lost as many games in any sport he played as he had since coming to the Giants. And he wondered if he could be responsible for the Giants' problems.

Owen was fired at the end of the 1953 season. Jim Lee Howell, a former Giant end and then a coach, replaced him. The first thing he did—and probably the wisest—was to go see Charlie.

He found him in Bowling Green, Missouri, about 5:30 one morning. Charlie and his boyhood friend Tony Malvezzi were selling liquid nitrogen fertilizer to farmers. Howell reached them as they were filling their tank trucks.

When Tony, the salesman of the pair, saw Howell, wearing a suit, tie, hat and topcoat, get out of his car, he intercepted him. "A guy dressed this well on a weekday; must be at least a 2,000 acre job. But when he asked for 'Chuck' instead of Roach he had to be from New York." (In the area of Mississippi around Clarksdale where Charlie was born, he is called Roach for some unfathomable reason because, typically, Charlie won't discuss it.)

Howell and Charlie talked briefly then and again that evening. Allie Sherman, who had been a backfield coach under Owen and was then a head coach in Canada, had contacted Charlie earlier. He promised $1,000 above any Giant offer.

Jim Lee started by promising Charlie a raise in salary. Charlie ignored the raise.

"Charlie, I need you," Jim Lee said. "If I try to get you the protection you need and some ends, will you give it another try?"

Charlie thought a moment. Then, "Okay, if you try, I'll try." Meanwhile, Tony, listening to his old buddy driving such a hard bargain, was waiting for Charlie to say something about more money, to dangle Sherman's offer as bait. He finally walked out of the room in frustration.

(Tony knew Charlie well. If pressed, Tony would have

acknowledged that Charlie had played football—with the exception of 1953—because he wanted to, not because of his paycheck. There were a lot of men like that in the NFL in those days. A newly married Raymond Berry, the Baltimore end who made himself great by his intense study of the game, which included close attention to game films, reportedly was asked one day if his bride could cook. Berry hesitated, then: "I don't know, but she can run a movie projector.")

Then came Vince Lombardi, loud, boisterous—and a man both Charlie and I grew to love.

Vince would be in charge of our offense. It was his first job in pro ball. He was 38. He had been a famous lineman at Fordham University, graduated cum laude and began to teach chemistry, Latin, and physics and coach football, baseball, and basketball at St. Cecilia's High School in Englewood, New Jersey. He intended to be a lawyer but six state football titles in eight years at St. Cecilia's brought him back to Fordham as freshman football coach. He had put in the T-formation at St. Cecilia's, did it again for the Fordham freshmen in 1947 and, the following year, for the Fordham varsity. Red Blaik then hired him as backfield coach for Army.

Vince served his pro apprenticeship with the Giants. He knew football, but he didn't know pro football. He brought three things: intelligence, excellent teaching skills, and a warmth and decency that attracted most people who met him.

Vince and Charlie approached each other warily. Charlie was suspicious of any rookie and, to him, Lombardi was a rookie. Vince was demonstrative and flamboyant and if you'd had a good game he'd come right into that locker room and plant a big kiss on your cheek. Charlie had never been exposed to that kind of coaching passion—nor did he care for it.

On the other hand, Charlie disappointed Vince—as he did any coach meeting him for the first time—by the terrible way he performed during training camp, a period he hated. Vince was full of fire and excitement and wanted every play in camp to be run as if it was a title game. Charlie, as usual, didn't think it was necessary and refused to work up a sweat. Vince knew that Howell had gone to Mississippi to get Charlie. He wasn't about to tell the Giant owners and the new head coach that Charlie wouldn't do as his quarterback.

All of us withheld our opinion on Vince. He was, then, just another successful college coach, and a very noisy one. We had all come out of college ball and we had learned how much different and harder the pro game was.

Vince sensed that and, perceptive man that he was, went out of his way to develop a rapport with our team. Although that rapport did not come quickly, it was Vince's major asset at the beginning, and throughout his career. He understood that he had a lot to learn too. So we taught each other. During training camp, Vince frequently came to the room Charlie and I shared to ask what we thought about the day's workouts. Kyle Rote usually was there and Lombardi would seek our opinions and listen to ideas we had. On the field, however, it was a different story. He ran the show and he ran it his way—in a firm, volatile, complete way.

Vince was a masterful teacher. A lot of coaches aren't; they may know what they want, but they can't show a younger player how to do it. Perhaps as a schoolteacher, Vince had become an extraordinary instructor. He made players of athletes who probably wouldn't have been able to stick in pro ball if they had been under another coach. He looked more for the desire to play and the capacity to learn than he did for physical skills.

At times he sounded more like a fourth grade math teacher than a coach. He'd get up to the blackboard and he'd say,

"All right, this is the 26 power play, 26 power play, do you have that, Eddie? 2, 6, 26 power play. Now the right guard *must* pull back, *must* pull back, the right guard *must* pull back, and he *has to pull back* to avoid the center who will be stepping to the on side. So the first step is back. Got that, Bill? The *first* step is back."

He drove us mad but when we went out on the field, we had it. And there was never a lot of complex stuff that we didn't need. He made it very simple and, soon, destructive— to other teams.

He made mistakes. He put in a "belly" series of plays, for example, where the quarterback sends the fullback off tackle, say, and depending on how the defensive end reacts, the quarterback either lets the fullback keep the ball or, if the end rushes in, he pulls the ball away and runs it himself or pitches out to his halfback. It was a forerunner to the option play. This worked at West Point. But it wouldn't work in pro ball. Your quarterback is a valuable asset and defensive ends are 6 feet 4 inches, 250 pounds and love to hit quarterbacks. A couple of hits and you're shopping for a new ball handler.

Vince didn't see this during those first weeks, so we all went along with it in practice. We ran it in dummy—non-contact—scrimmage to perfection. Charlie would fake to the fullback going off-tackle and then keep the ball himself. Of course, in dummy scrimmage the defensive end wouldn't hit Charlie. The end followed the fullback, Charlie took the ball away and pitched out to the halfback. It ran perfectly in dummy scrimmage and Vince would shout in great glee, "That's *it*, that's *it*. You've got it." Charlie would nod, we'd all smile and agree that it was the best play we'd ever seen. Then we would move into contact scrimmage.

Vince stood behind the offensive huddle. After Charlie had called a few of his own plays, Vince impatiently demanded, "Let's see that 47 belly now." Charlie would drawl quietly, "Coach I think we'd better work some more on the

26 power." Vince, still feeling his way, agreed reluctantly. The play ran and Vince called again, "Let's see that 47 belly *now*." Charlie would say, "I think we should work on the 49 sweep." And Vince would hesitate, then say, "Well, okay, right, right, the 49 sweep."

By that time, Charlie would be finished with his practice turn, his backup would come in, call the 47 belly and get killed by the defending end. During our first exhibition game under Lombardi against the Cardinals in Spokane, Vince repeatedly sent that play in, demanding that it be run. Charlie would listen to the message, call another play and somehow never find the "right moment" for the 47 belly. The play gradually disappeared.

When Vince installed the 49 sweep with the halfback following two guards around end, he wanted the guards to swing several yards behind their own line of scrimmage. That meant the left halfback—me—would have to swing back also to keep behind the guards who were blocking. You just can't move back that far in pro ball. The pursuit from the defensive team is too fast. The play was a sprint around end. The quicker the guards and the halfback could turn that corner, the quicker they could start making yardage. Vince was concerned about giving our tight end time to block the linebacker. He was afraid that if the linebacker were not taken out of the play, he would stack up the guards; the halfback would be stripped of his interference and could easily be stopped by the cornerback or the safety.

From the day Vince put the play on the blackboard, Charlie and I insisted that we couldn't give up those two or three yards. Vince had a tremendous amount of pride and a large ego. But if anyone went up to him privately to discuss something, he would always take time right there or in your room at night or, in later years, at his house. He was the kind of man who would listen.

Gradually, we started running the 49 sweep somewhere

between where Vince wanted it and where we knew it would work. We were both right. Opponents beat the 49 many times. But once we got a good block on the linebacker at the line of scrimmage, we were able to beat the pursuit around the corner. One guard went after the cornerback, the other protected to the inside and it was consistently the biggest gainer we had. It was also Lombardi's best play in both New York and Green Bay.

Vince changed my life. I had played two years with the Giants before he got there, on both defense and offense, never knowing from one game to another where I was going to be. I played wherever they didn't have someone else. I made All-Pro on offense and defense in 1953. I wasn't All-Pro. As far as I was concerned, I didn't even have a good year. Pittsburgh beat us and beat me twice for scores. Cleveland beat me for three touchdowns. I could say that I was exhausted. But actually, I was more embarrassed. I played more than 50 minutes during the last five games of that season. I could cover different receivers on two or three long passes, then the other team would punt and I'd run the punt back. The next play, I'd make an end run, fumble and go back to playing defense. I felt lost—and was. I began to question whether I belonged in pro ball.

His first day in training camp in 1954, Vince changed all that with three words: "You're my halfback." They were the most important words anybody ever said to me in football. I had never been anyone's halfback.

Even in college, I had played only one year on offense, my senior year. I had played on defense as a sophomore and junior. I made All-America my last year, but I never considered myself much of a football player. I knew I had gained 900 yards, but I still thought I was a better defensive back than offensive.

When Vince got to the Giants, I was exactly what Paul Hornung was when Vince got to Green Bay in 1959, a discouraged second-string back who was thinking of quitting. I was his Paul Hornung with the Giants. (Or, as I prefer to put it, Paul Hornung was his Frank Gifford with the Green Bay Packers.)

My talents fit Vince's concept of offensive football and he built his offense with the Giants, and later the Packers, around the left halfback. I could run. I could pass. I could catch passes and I could block. Vince carried enough from his single-wing days to realize that a versatile offense could be effective with the pros. Other coaches didn't want that. I don't think Tom Landry, had he become head coach when Owen left, would have wanted that. I don't think Paul Brown would have wanted that. Most good coaches want running backs to be running backs. They want receivers to be receivers and they want blockers to be blockers. Vince told Hornung in 1959 in essence what he had told me in 1954, and Hornung's pro career in effect began at that point—as did mine in 1954.

Would Hornung or I have been as effective playing for, say, Los Angeles as we were playing for Vince? If either of us had been with Los Angeles at the time when the Rams featured big backs and emphasis on speed and fast receivers. I don't know if we would even have played.

Howell, Lombardi and defensive player-coach Landry in 1954 immediately began to rebuild around a small core of Giants. By 1956 only nine men remained from the 1953 team: Dick Yelvington and Rosey Brown, offensive tackles; Bill Austin and Jack Stroud, offensive guards; Ray Wietecha, center; Em Tunnell, safety; Charlie, Kyle, and myself.

The Giants in 1954 traded for offensive end Bob Schnelker and linebacker Bill Svoboda. They drafted defensive back

Dick Nolan and signed linebacker Cliff Livingston and offensive end Ken MacAfee as free agents.

Rosey Grier, 280-pound defensive tackle; Mel Triplett, fullback; and Jim Patton, defensive back, were drafted in 1955. Alex Webster, named the Most Valuable Player in Canada in 1954, was lured to New York. The Giants traded for linebacker Harland Svare.

In 1956, New York drafted linebacker Sam Huff, punter Don Chandler, and defensive end Jim Katcavage. Defensive tackle Dick Modzelewski and defensive end Andy Robustelli came in trades.

The heart of the team that was to be the best in Giant history was set. The club would win the conference and league championship in 1956, the first time for New York since 1938 and not repeated to this day. Conference titles came in bunches, in 1958, '59, and, bolstered by new faces, in '61, '62 and '63.

It was a memorable line-up that included:

Defensively, Modzelewski and Rosey Grier at the tackles; Robustelli and Katcavage at the ends; Svare, Svoboda and Huff, linebackers; Tunnell, Nolan, Gene Filipski and Patton in the secondary.

Offensively, Rote and Schnelker at the ends; Yelvington and Brown at the tackles; Austin and Stroud, guards; Wietecha, center; Webster and me at the halfbacks; Triplett, fullback, and Charlie.

Average age: 25.

Only one major element was missing—a deep threat—and the Giants didn't get that until end-flanker Del Shofner, who ran the 100 in 9.7, came with Y.A. Tittle at the beginning of 1961.

Periodically, Vince's blunt, straight-out method of coaching backfired on him. We had a player who was sensitive to criticism. He did well as long as no one complicated his existence. We were watching films one day of the previous game. We had lost and Vince saw several frames of the film that showed this guy run right past a linebacker, his blocking assignment. The linebacker almost decapitated the ball carrier, Alex Webster.

It had been happening fairly often and Vince seized on these few frames and started running them back and forth on the projector, shouting, "Smith (and I use the name "Smith" to protect the guilty), *look at yourself,* Smith. Smith, hear me? Smith. Smith," and he kept running those frames back and forth for what seemed like minutes and then "Smith," a tough southern boy sitting in the back of the room, said very softly, "Run that one more time, coach, and I'll cut you." Vince suspected, as did the rest of us, that this guy carried a knife with him all the time. He hit the forward button on the projector and didn't say another word.

But Vince was a genius at motivating his players, and game films was one device he used well. He often would stop the projector to focus attention on a good—or bad—move. "Here we were, all college men," Packer guard Jerry Kramer said years later, "and he'd use something as basic as that. 'He's psyching me,' you'd say to yourself, but damned if it wasn't effective.

"I remember one particular block I made." Kramer continued. "It was against Chicago and I pulled out and got Bennie McRae, the cornerback. I . . . knocked him flat on his rear. I stepped over and picked off the defensive end cutting across and then I headed downfield, but by that time the runner had made his cut and was gone.

"Two days later when it came on the screen, Lombardi started yelling, 'Hey, that's a helluva block, watch this' and he ran it over and over again. I don't believe a single word was written on it in the newspapers but all the ballplayers saw it. You've got to have that."

Vince loved practical jokes, especially when they were on him. He was a fanatic about dummy scrimmage. It had to be done just so. While the offensive team was running against the defensive group, the rest of the players were just standing watching and waiting for their turn. Each of us would have to run about 10 yards when it was our time to work and, as practice wore on, we got tired of standing.

We gradually moved closer and closer to the two teams working out until we were almost on top of them. This infuriated Vince, so we began to do it purposely. We'd keep inching up and he'd stomp around and wave us back. After about the third time he'd scream, "Get back, get back, stop crowding the offense."

One day, he saw an old beat-up orange peel that had been lying on the field for lord knows how long. He said, "Everyone behind the orange peel. Anyone who passes the orange peel gets a lap around the field." This sounded so silly that we lined up single file behind the orange peel. He turned around and saw that and roared. Then we all scattered and every time he turned to watch the play, we'd push the orange peel closer and pretty soon we were right back on top of him. He turned around, began to shout, "I told you guys to get behind the orange . . . ," looked down and there was the orange peel. These were the things that would delight him and crack him up.

We were a smart ball club and we came to know each other's talents and personalities to an extraordinary degree. Charlie was the kind of man who wanted information brought back to the huddle because no quarterback can see everything going on downfield. If I'm wide to the left, the only way Charlie would have of knowing how that back was covering me on a certain situation would be to ask me.

In the huddle when Charlie called a play. I'd be on his left, Alex Webster on his right, and Kyle on my left. We faced the offensive linemen and three or four of us might have something to say. Charlie would start by calling a play and I might say, "I'll run a circle-in on it, hold the middle linebacker," and Kyle might add, "Down and in won't work this time, I'll take it down and out." ("Circle-in" and "down and out" were pass patterns we would run.) While that was going on, Rosey Brown and Ray Wietecha might be suggesting altered blocking assignments. All of this would take a matter of four or five seconds. And it all started when Charlie called a play, listened to our suggestions, accepted them and then said, "Okay, on three." Many times, of course, he was definite about what he wanted and waved off advice with his hand.

Sometimes, if one of us had a play in mind, to save time we would tell Charlie returning to the huddle and if he agreed he would simply say, "Call it." Kyle was playing split end to the left against Cleveland one afternoon; it was late in the game and he had been running decoy patterns with the action going over to the right side involving the tight end and the flanker. Kyle had noticed that the back assigned to cover him was drifting more and more to the inside. He outlined the play in the following code: "Brown right, IX right, flood right, L zig out." (The brown right told the team what formation the play was to run from. IX right told the right end and flanker they would run a crossing pattern. Flood right told the setbacks they were to circle and flare to the right, and L zig out was the route Kyle was to run.) Charlie simply asked, "Got it? On two." It worked for a touchdown.

A lot of teams and quarterbacks couldn't do that, particularly younger teams or quarterbacks with ego problems. But few things distracted Charlie; he knew who could make a contribution—and who was just talking. On any club, there are ends who are "always" open, backs who "could score a touchdown if you just gave me the ball." On Charlie's team we had none of this.

The difference between 1953 and 1954 was almost too dramatic. For the first time in Charlie's professional career, he had a coach who was all offense and who wanted a fundamental running game because that would keep the other team sufficiently off balance to allow passes to succeed. With that new philosophy *and* passing protection now, Charlie threw 20 touchdown passes against three in 1953.

I think we could have won our conference title in Vince's first year. We were leading our conference in the ninth game of the season when Kyle and I collided and were knocked out. I ripped ligaments in my right knee and was done for the rest of the season. Kyle missed two games. The Rams beat us by one point and put us out of first place. Then Charlie was hurt and finished for the year. We lost three of the last four games.

The Giants got off to a disastrous start in 1955. We lost five of our first seven games, then turned around to win four straight and tie one. That's when we realized we were turning into a good club.

By the time training camp started for 1956, Vince had become the best offensive coach in the game. His apprenticeship was over. He knew his offensive team and what it could do. We had long since realized Vince's ability. Charlie was by now one of his favorite players, both on and off the field. Frequently, Charlie, Kyle, and I would go over to Vince's house in New Jersey and study game films and talk football until Vince's wife, Marie, threw us out.

Vince was a solid, fundamental coach, but he also loved deception. He coached much as he played bridge, a game he loved. He could win a trick by playing an ace or a king, but he'd rather finesse the queen. He would have an emotional orgasm when he did. Or sit and glower when he couldn't. Same thing on the field. Football basics, but always a trick or two.

We were studying movies of games with Pittsburgh in Vince's basement one night when Charlie realized that whenever we ran our sweep to the left side, Dick Albans, the Pittsburgh cornerback on that side, ignored his key, the pulling guard, and raced in to stop the run. So we designed several plays just for him. On the first play from scrimmage the next Sunday, Charlie called a fake sweep left for Alex Webster. I was flanked left in the sweep formation. I raced upfield as if to block Albans, but stepped around him as he came up to make the tackle. (Just like in the movies.) Charlie hit me for 67 yards and a score.

We kicked off to Pittsburgh, they fumbled and we had the ball on their 35. Charlie called the same formation, this time built on a fake off-tackle run by Mel Triplett. I was out wide again. Charlie faked to Triplett, hid the ball on his hip and Albans came in like a rocket to stop Triplett. I just got out of his way and caught Charlie's pass for another touchdown. Those two plays won what turned into a typical New York-Pittsburgh dogfight.

The Giants easily took the 1956 conference championship. It was the first time Cleveland had not won the title since it entered the NFL in 1950.

The Giants tore through the Bears in the league championship game, 47–7. It was no contest. The field was frozen and the Giants wore sneakers brought in by Andy Robustelli, who owned a sporting goods store.

Charlie, like all fine quarterbacks, instinctively "knew" what his primary and secondary receivers would do when problems occurred. During the title game with the Bears, we had scored an early touchdown because we were able to take advantage of a rookie back. In the fourth quarter, we tried the play again, a down-and-in pattern to me; but this time, the rookie had been replaced, and the new cornerback read the play correctly and would have stopped it. I broke the pattern, kept running straight downfield and Charlie caught me with a 29-yard pass that set up another score. I ignored a fundamental rule—don't cross up your quarterback—when I ran behind the man covering me. Had Charlie thrown to where I should have gone, the cornerback could have intercepted for a long runback, possibly a touchdown. But I knew Charlie. I knew he would read the same thing I read.

Wrote one reporter after that game: "Conerly, the man they had booed into retirement, completed seven of 10 passes for 195 yards and called a near-perfect game." He could have left out the "near."

The following year we were 7 and 2, then lost the last three games, none by more than 11 points. It was Jimmy Brown's rookie year and he ran for 942 yards to bring Cleveland the eastern conference championship. The Browns beat us twice that season.

Writer Paul Zimmerman once quoted an old coach as saying, "Never mind how many passes he throws and what his completion average looks like, my quarterback's got to be the guy who can take you in in the last two minutes when it's getting dark and the fans are booing and the wind is blowing and there's so much ice on the ball he can't grip it."

In 1958, Charlie Conerly, age 38, fulfilled those specifications.

We started out badly, losing two of our first five games. Then it was Cleveland and Jimmy Brown. Booed only two weeks before when a sluggish team couldn't do anything right, Charlie passed for three touchdowns to give Cleveland its first loss, 21–17. (Charlie's three touchdown passes that day gave him 140 for his career, second only at that time to Sammy Baugh's 187.) He accomplished that job in the face of a brutally punishing afternoon from the Browns' defensive line. The game was the turning point in the most exhausting stretch drive I was ever in.

Baltimore, also unbeaten, was next. They were leading, 21–14, in the third period when Charlie moved us 58 yards in nine plays. The tying touchdown came on a diving catch by Kyle in the corner of the end zone. Pat Summerall then kicked the winning field goal with 1:59 left.

We had upset the best two teams in pro football. Charlie had completed 24 of 40 passes, four for touchdowns. He saw none of those scores. Each time, he was buried under defensive linemen.

We flew home from Cleveland. By the time we arrived at La Guardia Airport, Charlie could hardly walk off the plane.

"He looked as if he had been in a fight," Perian told me the next day. "His left leg was one solid red mass from cleat marks. Somebody else had ripped his nose right near his eye with a fingernail."

Two weeks later Pittsburgh upset us. We had to win the last four games on the schedule just to tie for the conference lead and force a playoff. We did it, coming from behind in the last two games.

Cleveland was last on our schedule and the Browns needed just a tie to take the conference title. We had to win the game and, if we did, then beat Cleveland again in a playoff for the conference championship.

Jimmy Brown broke away on the first play for 65 yards and a touchdown on a snow- and ice-covered field. We trailed at the half, 10–3.

But we had noticed that Cleveland's secondary, anticipating the run, had overshifted when I tried an option pass to Alex Webster. When the Giants recovered a fumble in the last period on Cleveland's 45, Charlie called the option play again. He faked to Webster, gave it to me and I ran to the right as if the play was going to be a run. The secondary overcommitted itself again and I passed to Kyle, racing down the left sideline. He reached the six. We scored minutes later on the same play, this time when I faked a pass to Kyle and threw to Bob Schnelker in the end zone. We were tied, 10–10.

That was all Cleveland needed for the conference title, but Pat Summerall made the difference for us.

Kicking with a sprained knee, Pat had missed a field goal from the 31 late in the fourth quarter. He got another chance in one of the most dramatic moments in Giant history. The ball was on the Brown's 49-yard line. (Actually no one was sure. The field was covered with snow. We couldn't see the yard markers. I think it was 51 yards.) The lights went on. Dusk and snowflakes the size of half dollars began to obliterate vision. With slightly more than two minutes left and a conference title riding with Pat, he kicked it perfectly.

The Giant defense held Jimmy Brown to 18 yards in the following week's playoff and we won, 10–0. The touchdown came on a double reverse from the Cleveland nine that was supposed to end with me running between right tackle and end. Confronted by a pileup, I turned, saw Charlie trailing the play all by himself and tossed the ball to him. He was shocked but kept running into the end zone. He had a word for me on the way back to the bench: "Next time I give you the ball, pal, you keep it." (In deference to Perian, I've left out the adjectives.) During the locker room celebration, we told the curious press that was the way the play was supposed to go while our Mississippi friend tried to look modest.

Now Baltimore, comparatively rested from having clinched its conference title early and then having two weeks off, was back for the NFL championship game. It was to be the first overtime sudden-death title game in the history of the league. Some called it the best game ever played. It was not that.

(A case *can* be made for it being the most important game played for professional football. Only two years before, seven thousand seats were empty when we won the league title, an index to public interest in the sport then. In the "sudden-death" game, however, Yankee Stadium was jammed and millions remained in front of their television sets. America and the world of advertising "discovered" pro football that day. The extraordinary success of New York—center of the advertising industry—in winning four conference titles in the next five years helped significantly.)

I fumbled twice in the first half (so obviously it couldn't have been the greatest game ever played). Both fumbles led to Baltimore scores. At the half, we were down, 14–3.

Early in the third period the Colts drove to our three-yard line, first and goal. Our defense held, the first time Baltimore had been stopped inside the 10 all season.

We took the ball on our five. Now we had the momentum and Charlie moved us in a comeback that, on any normal day, would have been enough.

Johnny Unitas is remembered for bringing Baltimore from behind to win. But it was Charlie's work that afternoon that forced the overtime.

On our third play, Charlie hit Rote at the Giants' 30-yard line and Kyle raced to midfield before he was hit—and fumbled. Webster scooped up the ball and reached the one-yard line. Triplett scored on the next play. The score: Baltimore 14, Giants 10.

The Colts were overshifting whenever we lined up in a strong-right formation. Charlie, who had been throwing all day to Kyle and me, first switched to end Bob Schnelker, hitting him twice in succession—for 17 yards and 46 yards. On the Baltimore 15, Charlie put the team into the strong-right line-up. Baltimore again overshifted. Conerly faked to the right end, MacAfee, and threw to me near the left sideline on the five and I scored easily. We led, 17–14.

Our defense forced Baltimore to punt. Minutes later we had the ball. Third and four on our own 39. With little more than two minutes remaining in the game, people preparing to leave, and sportswriters voting for the game's Most Valuable Player, Charlie sent me on a sweep around right end. Gino Marchetti, Colt end, had fought off Schnelker's block, so I cut inside. Marchetti grabbed me and then 285 pounds of Big Daddy Lipscomb leaped on both of us. Marchetti's ankle snapped and he screamed.

I had the first down. That would have meant the ball game and the league championship. But the referee picked up the ball and held it rather than mark the spot. He started to pull players off the injured Marchetti. He then marked the ball a couple of inches short of a first down. It was fourth down on our own 43. Because our defense had manhandled Baltimore for the entire second half, coach Jim Lee Howell called for a punt. Don Chandler hit a beauty to the Baltimore 14.

Johnny Unitas had 1:58 remaining. Passing to Lenny Moore once and to Berry three times for short yardage, Unitas reached the Giant 13 with seven seconds left. Steve Myhra, whose first-quarter try at a field goal had been blocked when Modzelewski pulled Colt tackle Art Donovan aside and Huff vaulted through the hole, this time made it. The game was tied—and "over."

But under the league ruling, we entered sudden-death overtime. The first team to score would win.

We received the kickoff. I carried for four yards to the 23. Two plays later, Charlie, receiver covered, scrambled and was stopped inches short of a first down.

The momentum changed again—now, irretrievably, against us.

Unitas, back on his own 20 following Chandler's punt, took 13 plays, including two passes to Berry for 33 yards, to score.

Charlie called and played a superb game. Sportswriters had already voted him the game's Most Valuable Player; they had to vote again when Unitas drove his team twice to win. (With the honor went a Corvette. "For months afterward," sighed Perian, "I had nightmares about Dorothy Unitas driving gaily around Baltimore in 'my' Corvette.")

The Giants kept drafting collegiate quarterbacks, three or four of them All-Americans, during Charlie's tenure—Travis Tidwell of Alabama, Fred Benners of Southern Methodist, Bobby Clatterbuck of Houston, Arnold Galiffa of Army, George Shaw of Oregon, Don Heinrich of Washington and Lee Grosscup of Utah—but over his 14-year career none could dislodge him.

Even his roommate tried to get his job. I wrote Jim Lee Howell a letter during the '58–'59 offseason asking for a trial at quarterback during training camp and the preseason exhibition games. It took me three days to write the letter. I had been a single-wing tailback in high school, and a backup quarterback playing defense in college. With the Giants, I threw frequently from the option play. It was not greatly different from the quarterback roll-out or drop-back moves. Because I could run as well as throw, I thought I could help diversify our attack. After Jim Lee agreed to a preseason trial, I went to Clarksdale to tell Charlie. We were fishing at the time I told him, but I don't think I overly distressed him.

I think Charlie was amused by my tryout at his job. Two days before we had to report to training camp in Burlington, Vermont, Charlie and I drove to the New Jersey shore to visit restaurateur Toots Shor at his summer home. The second night, the three of us decided to go to Atlantic City where Frank Sinatra was opening. Toots' car was an extension of his bar. A 15-minute drive became 90 minutes when his driver became lost. By the time we reached the night club, the three of us had depleted the liquor supply somewhat. The entrance to the club was packed with people looking for show business stars. Up we come, the door of the limousine opens and out roll a couple of bottles onto the road. We attracted some attention. Everyone ran over asking each other, "Who's that? Who's that?"

They didn't get Natalie Wood. Charlie, first out, drew himself erect and responded to the group proudly, "That," pointing to me, "is the New York Football Giants' quarterback."

The evening proceeded. After the show, we returned to Toots' home. For a reason I choose to forget, we began to play football in his living room. Charlie was the center and I was going to show Toots how I could play quarterback. The game ended abruptly when Toots fell down a flight of stairs.

We raced to New York early the next morning holding our heads and caught a flight to Burlington. Wellington Mara, the Giants' owner, picked us up at the airport.

"How was Sinatra's show?" he asked innocently.

Charlie and I looked at each other. How did Wellington know we were there? Seems our arrival in Atlantic City had made the wire services.

Howell and I had agreed that any time he felt the experiment wouldn't work, I would return to halfback. I started two exhibition games at quarterback, one against the Eagles and the second in the next to last preseason game against Detroit. We would have been leading the Lions at halftime if my receiver hadn't dropped a pass on the goal line. During the intermission, Jim Lee asked me to return to halfback. He had, I suspect, been humoring me. We had a championship team and I was his leading rusher and receiver. He saw no reason to shake up the club.

Spurred undoubtedly by the challenge, Charlie became the Most Valuable Player in the league that season. Although we were defending conference champions in 1959, teams we played in exhibitions were seemingly unimpressed by our scoring ability. This bothered Allie Sherman, who rejoined the team that year as Vince Lombardi's successor when Vince became head coach in Green Bay. Sherman asked Charlie to throw frequently and long in the season opener against Los Angeles.

Charlie quickly passed us into a 17–0 lead. When the Rams scored three times to move in front, Charlie returned to the game. He moved the Giants 74 yards with five consecutive passes to set up a field goal by Summerall. The Rams still led by one. With three minutes left, Charlie passed on fourth and 11 on our own 45. He hit Schnelker on the Los Angeles 20. Summerall kicked the winning field goal three plays later for a 23–21 win.

Charlie completed 21 of 31 passes for 321 yards. The writers: "Conerly was . . . never better. . . . Most of his connections in the last half were made with two or more Rams dangling . . . from his neck. Yet (no passes) were intercepted." The Ram game was only the beginning of Charlie's most successful season.

By the end of the year, he was an almost unanimous choice by NFL players as the league's Most Valuable Player. He had completed 113 of 194 passes for 1,706 yards, 14 touchdowns and only four interceptions.

By 1960, changes had occurred. Tom Landry would leave at the end of the season to become head coach in Dallas. Jim Lee had served notice that 1960 would be his last season. Alex Webster, who had gained an average 500 yards rushing during each of the previous five seasons, ripped knee ligaments in an exhibition game and sat out most of the year. Charlie was hurt early.

New York was 3–1–1 heading into Cleveland's Municipal Stadium jammed with almost 89,000 spectators. Playing with a badly swollen ankle and elbow, changing half of his plays at the line of scrimmage, Charlie led us to a 17–13 upset.

The following week against Pittsburgh, playing with the same injuries and a knee injured early in the game—he didn't tell anyone until the game was over and played in agonizing pain—Charlie brought the team back from a 14–0 deficit to lead, 17–14. The Steelers scored 10 points to go ahead in the fourth quarter.

Conerly limped back on the field, passed for one touchdown, and, after an interception gave New York the ball, brought the team close enough for Summerall to kick the winning field goal, 27–24. During that drive, with his receivers covered, Charlie scrambled twice—for 16 yards and then for 17—in spite of the pain from his multiple injuries.

Charlie played part-time the rest of the season. Kyle was injured and, later, Jim Katcavage. I was forced out for the last four games and all of 1961 when I was hurt during the Philadelphia game the following week.

Quarterbacks are highly overrated, both in defeat and victory. Many in the media put too much of the blame on the quarterback for a loss and too much of the praise on him when his team wins. It's sharply out of proportion in both directions.

You can take an average quarterback, put him with a great football team and he might go undefeated. But put a great quarterback with an average football team and he's going to lose a lot of games.

All the fine quarterbacks played with superb teams. Johnny Unitas didn't make Big Daddy Lipscomb or Bill Pellington. He also had a Raymond Berry and Lenny Moore to throw to and Moore and Alan Ameche to run and an excellent offensive line. He was an exceptional quarterback. But put him with the same team I played with in 1953 and no one would know how to spell his name yet.

Quarterbacks are important and they can be exciting. A Joe Namath can have a sensational night and lose, 38–24. He still lost, but in a more dramatic way. A Namath can lift a team to a degree, but you can't expect him to do it week in and week out and he doesn't.

I thought Bill Nelson was a fine quarterback. Every bit as good as, say, Bart Starr, who will probably be in the Hall of Fame some day. But Nelson played with the Pittsburgh Steelers when they were a poor club. He played with the Cleveland Browns when they were on the bottom. And he got beat up fairly well. He probably could match knee operations with Namath three for one. If Nelson had been with the Packers when they were winning, I believe Green Bay would have just done as well. This is not a putdown of Bart. It's just a fact, overlooked by the media in search of a glamorous focal point.

The same media wondered before the 1975 Super Bowl: Can Fran Tarkenton beat the Steelers? Sure he could have done it—if Ron Yary could have controlled Dwight White, if Milt Sunde could have handled Joe Greene, if Chuck Foreman could have broken loose on a kickoff and run it back for a touchdown, if the defense had given him the ball in good field position; sure, then Fran could have won the game. The same story was true of Roger Staubach in 1976. He didn't lose the game. He just couldn't win it.

That's the reason I just stopped thinking for a moment and hit that guy outside the Polo Grounds in 1953. I became so furious that he would pick out one man and blame him for everything that went on with 22 players.

Charlie was the same quarterback in 1959 when he led the league in passing and was named Most Valuable Player that he was in 1952 and 1953.

The Giants put a team around him in the interim, an offensive line so he didn't get his teeth shoved down his throat and had time to throw, a simplified but superb offense, an extraordinary defense, and suddenly people were shocked because Charlie Conerly was a great quarterback.

One of these days the media group that elects members to

the pro Hall of Fame will look at Charlie, ignore the statistics, consider the players he was working with and what he accomplished, and realize that he was one of the great quarterbacks of all time.

You can't get into the Hall of Fame when they base it on statistics if you didn't have someone to help you get the numbers. Otto Graham had Dante Lavelli and Mac Speedie; Waterfield had Hirsch and Fears.

Look who Charlie played with. His leading receiver was a lead-footed halfback. Me. I was the only receiver he had in the league's top 10 after 1949. But I don't know how many times I was pulled down from behind on long runs because I just wasn't fast enough. Kyle was an extraordinary receiver, but it's a wonder he played as long and as well as he did with two terribly injured knees. If Charlie had had Lenny Moore or Del Shofner for more of his career he'd have won a lot more games and the Giants probably would have won league championships in '54, '57, '58, and '59.

The Giants during Charlie's time were never a passing team in any sense, in part because we lacked the game-breaking receiver. When Charlie was elected Most Valuable Player in 1959, he averaged only nine passes a game. We had Webster, Triplett and me running out of the backfield. We didn't use a flanker as a special player until 1955 because we didn't have one. We had an option play with Kyle or me running or throwing. Charlie really didn't throw that much.

Statistics *are* important and by that yardstick he doesn't qualify for the Hall of Fame. But that's only one criterion. Charlie was far more valuable to the teams he played with, teams with personnel much less skilled than the players, say, Y.A. Tittle played with. Y.A. is in the Hall of Fame and justly so. But Y.A. never won a conference or league title in San Francisco. Then he came to New York and had three extraordinary years with different talent. The "supporting cast" can't be ignored. Someday O.J. Simpson undoubtedly will be in the Hall of Fame. But he should take guards Reggie McKenzie and Joe DeLamielleure and the rest of the offensive line in with him. O.J. agrees. He's said it many times but no one listens.

By the time the 1961 season began, 16 of the 36-man Giant squad were new to the club.

Y.A. Tittle was brought to New York from San Francisco by Wellington Mara and the new head coach, Allie Sherman, just before the season started as help for Charlie, but he soon became the starting quarterback. Aided immensely by Shofner and a new tight end, Joe Walton, Y.A. led the Giants to a conference title.

"As Y.A. tightened his grasp on the starting job by virtue of one outstanding performance after another, Charlie's reaction was to study harder," Perian said. "He pored over his play book at night as if he were the only quarterback. . . . He was itching to play, but he didn't sulk. Neither did he pretend. When acquaintances sought to gloss over the situation by remarking, 'I know you're glad the Giants have someone who can give you a little rest,' Charlie refused to let the convenient pretext pass. [He has a proclivity for uncomfortable honesty that I lack.] 'That's not why I haven't been playing,' he would say. 'Tittle's doing a great job and I can't get him out of there.' "

Y.A. twice needed help badly from Charlie. Conerly came into the sixth game, against the Rams, with 17 minutes left and the Giants behind, 14–10. Nothing Y.A. was doing that day was working. Charlie scored two touchdowns quickly on passes to Shofner and to Rote. He called his own number and slipped off-tackle for a key first down on the Rams' 10, setting up the pass to Kyle.

In the next-to-last game of the season, against Philadelphia, the Giants immediately fell behind. The Giants and Eagles were tied for first place in the conference. The winner undoubtedly would go on to get the title.

Sherman sent Charlie in midway through the second quarter with the Giants trailing, 10–7. New York scored on the first play. Shofner and Rote had been drawing double coverage. Charlie ordered Shofner deep to clear the left side of defenders, sent Walton underneath Shofner and hit him for a 35-yard touchdown. Charlie threw two more touchdown passes in the second half, both to Shofner, to edge Philadelphia, 28–24.

Charlie's "vice": he wasn't colorful. He did his work brilliantly, consistently, over a longer period as a starting quarterback than all but one man during his era. He could have gone on, I believe, at age 40—and perhaps beyond—with the receivers New York assembled that year. But when Y.A. secured the starting spot, Charlie didn't argue. He saved the title with two clutch jobs—and then retired and, characteristically, left without a lot of noise. His pride wouldn't let him be number two.

And why should he have to be?

Y.A.
Tittle

"I always felt that any day someone was going to take my job. I'm not so sure that I ever thought I had arrived. Even in the good years I never held out for salary; they may not have wanted me. I worked 'hungry' until the day I quit playing ball."

It seems strange when I think back to the years when the New York Giants were the best team in professional football under Charlie Conerly and Y.A. Tittle that Y.A., hero of so many fall and winter afternoons, had not always been a star, had in fact been hooted and benched in San Francisco and, finally, given away.

Early in the spring of 1961, the San Francisco 49ers were trying to trade Tittle, their starting quarterback since 1952. But no one wanted him. An attempted deal with Los Angeles collapsed. The Giants weren't interested. Conerly was healthy after hurting his arm and knee in 1960 and the coaches wanted to develop Lee Grosscup as his backup.

Y.A. was the fourth leading passer in the National Football League in yardage gained at that point. But the 49ers' coaching staff had lost faith in him. Quarterback John Brodie was the new boy in town and he was pushing Y.A. hard.

The 1960 season had been an unhappy one for Y.A. He

and Brodie had alternated as starting quarterback for most of
the year. Then, hit hard by a Chicago linebacker with three
games left to play, Y.A. pulled a groin muscle. He was finished
for the season.

Coach Red Hickey at that point installed an offense called
the shotgun, a variant of the old single wing. The quarterback,
now called a tailback, played about six yards behind the center. He had to handle the ball, pass and run. Y.A. ran like an
aging member of the DAR. The shotgun was designed for
backs like Brodie and Billy Kilmer, All-American from
UCLA, a good runner and passer drafted by Hickey after the
1960 season ended. It wasn't Y.A.'s type of offense. He knew
it. The press knew it. The fans and the entire NFL knew it.
Y.A. was being written off.

"The offseason between 1960 and 1961 was a terrible ordeal for me," Y.A. said. "I was torn between two emotions:
hurt pride and determination with perhaps a little anger
thrown in. My pride had been damaged because of the way I
had finished the 1960 season, riding the bench with an injury,
completely lost in the hysteria of the shotgun, the 'new trend'
in pro football offense.

"People knew I had been injured but no one seemed to remember it. They didn't recall that I had been the 49ers' starting quarterback against Chicago the day I was injured. Or that
I had been San Francisco's starting quarterback since 1952.
Or that I had been a starting pro quarterback for 13 years.

"All they talked about was 'Tittle benched.'

"At times I said, 'The hell with it. Quit that damned game.
You've been at it too long anyway. You've got an insurance
business that can support your family.'

"But the next instant, I'd get stubborn: 'Come back for another season and show them you're still a good quarterback.'"

As offseason rumors spread about Y.A. being traded, he
confronted the issue and went to see Hickey.

"Where do I stand with your team, Red?" he asked.

"I'm going to be honest, Y.A. We might make a trade for you if we can work things out with Los Angeles."

"That's good," Tittle replied, "because I'll retire if you try to trade me back east. But what if you can't make a deal?"

"We're planning to go all the way with the shotgun. If you *want* to play more football, you'll just have to come to training camp and take your chances."

The pride of not being number one hit Y.A. and his confidence in himself. After years of being part of the San Francisco organization, Y.A. suddenly felt alone and on the outside. It had been his ball club; now it no longer wanted or needed him.

Then the whispers began—among the team and in some papers: Tittle is almost 35. Maybe it's time for him to retire.

In August 1961, when training camp began for the new season, both Y.A. and the 49ers were still undecided concerning his future. Unwilling to give his position away, Y.A. reported to camp.

The groin muscle still hurt. Tittle didn't want anyone to know it, so each day before practice, he went into a toilet stall in the camp bathroom with a roll of tape and a roll of bandage and secretly wrapped his leg, flushing the toilet to conceal the sound every time he had to rip off a strip of tape.

His passing during training camp was superb—working out of the T-formation. Then the Giants arrived for the first exhibition game. Brodie started with the shotgun formation. The Giant defense stopped the shotgun and led, 21–13, going into the fourth quarter.

Hickey sent Tittle in with the T-formation. Y.A. moved San Francisco 67 yards in seven plays to score. San Francisco now was one point down. When the 49ers got the ball next, Tittle marched the team 75 yards in four plays, then hit Monte Stickles in the end zone in the final minutes but the play was nullified by a San Francisco penalty.

With that one quarter, Tittle had become an embarrassment

to Hickey. Red didn't want Y.A. and the T-formation around for the press and fans to use as second-guessing material once the season started.

Meanwhile, Grosscup had been disappointing in training camp and the Giants now were looking for a backup quarterback to Conerly. They were impressed by Tittle in the exhibition game. The deal was made. Y.A. was virtually given away. He was traded for a rookie lineman, Leo Cordileone. (Cordileone's wisecrack when he heard about the trade drew laughs around the NFL for years: "Just Tittle? Is that all they got for me? Just Tittle?")

Even then, Y.A. almost was not taken by the Giants. "I remember sitting in several meetings with the other coaches and arguing that he could help us a lot," Don Heinrich, the Giants' backfield coach, told me. "Some of the coaches didn't think Tittle had much left."

Y.A. was angry. He would have hated to retire at that point —"benched and traded"—but what awaited him in New York? Charlie Conerly had been the league's best passer and Most Valuable Player two years before and had led the Giants to three conference titles and one league championship within the past five years.

Y.A. had no idea how the groin injury would heal. He was very much a family man—he and Minnette then had three children—and it would have been difficult to move them so close to the start of a new school year. But he didn't want to leave them.

Benched and then traded for a rookie lineman. It hurt. Y.A. decided to quit.

He says I was the one who persuaded him to change his mind. Maybe so. When I heard of the trade, I called him to do a telephone interview for my radio show. I reached him just as he returned home from the San Francisco training camp. After we had taped the segment, Y.A. began to interrogate me. He didn't want to come to New York to sit on the bench.

"Charlie's my best friend," I told him. "But he needs help. You'll play and you and Charlie can win with this team."

Allie Sherman, who had just been named to succeed Jim Lee Howell as Giant coach, called Y.A. shortly after I did. He also told Tittle he would play.

Y.A.'s coming to New York took courage. Y.A. was highly respected by players but had never been considered a star in San Francisco. He had drawn boos there in recent years. He could easily fall on his face with the new club. There was enormous precedent for that. It was a gloomy-looking future for Colonel Slick, as I later affectionately referred to him. But I had meant what I said. I knew that the man I'd watched, admired, and played against for years had a lot of football left.

At that point, New York didn't have Del Shofner, who would join with Y.A. to form one of the outstanding pass-receiving teams in league history. Kyle Rote and I for several years had been New York's leading pass receivers. I had retired following a head injury in 1960 and Kyle was 34.

Why *did* Tittle go to the Giants? While he admits that I was persuasive, there was a lot to consider before he reversed his decision to give it all up. Quarterbacks who had started pro ball the same year as he—Johnny Lujack, Charlie Trippi, Harry Gilmer—all had retired. Why go to back up an established and popular quarterback and inflict again the mental and physical punishment and the severe asthma attacks that made special medication for him part of the team doctor's on-field equipment?

Knowing Y.A. as I do now, his decision probably hung on his pride and the fact that if he retired, his family's last memory of his football days would be the insult of the trade.

The next day, Y.A. flew to the Giants' training camp in Salem, Oregon. His fears of failure, his self-doubt didn't show, but he had to be concerned about his future in a game that for Tittle had begun nearly a quarter of a century earlier.

By the age of 11, Y.A. was already a "thrower." By his senior year in high school in Marshall, Texas, he was second team all-state tailback. Who beat him? Another senior, Bobby Layne of Dallas. Layne of course went on to a legendary career at the University of Texas and Detroit.

Y.A. accepted what amounted to an athletic scholarship from Louisiana State University. But on graduation day, Blair Cherry, an assistant coach at the University of Texas, came to Marshall with several other assistants and virtually kidnapped him. Y.A. drove off with them. The plan was to tuck him away in summer school, get him a job and hide him from LSU counterspies.

In that war year, the navy had taken over the school's dormitories so Y.A. found himself in Mrs. Poole's Boarding House. In the adjacent room was Bobby Layne. Suddenly, Y.A. found there was a world beyond Marshall, Texas.

"I'd never been far out of Marshall in my life," he told me years later. "Our county and all the adjacent counties but one were dry. Layne was a grown man compared to me.

"He was drinking beer and playing poker all night for big stakes and dating girls. I was just learning how to play poker. I never drank beer in my life.

"Even during the summer, he was the 'big' freshman on campus. I was intimidated. I couldn't compete socially. I didn't look forward to competing for the tailback job with him. After three weeks, I was sorry I had gone to Texas."

Magically, LSU line coach Red Swanson appeared in Austin, home of the University of Texas, and called Y.A. They came to terms without delay. But Swanson would not leave unless Y.A. called Texas head coach Dana X. Bible to tell him he was quitting.

"I can't call *him*," Tittle protested. Bible was then one of the most famous coaches in the country.

"We're not going to take you unless you do," Swanson said.

He gave Y.A. some change. Y.A. walked over to a nearby telephone booth, faked a call and conversation, came back, said Coach Bible was out but he had left a message with Mrs. Bible and she understood perfectly.

Freshmen then were eligible for the varsity. Y.A. started immediately. The offense was changed from a single wing to the T-formation before his sophomore season and Tittle fit into the "T" as though it had been designed for him personally. He set a number of LSU passing records—most of which lasted until 1972.

Tittle also played defense at LSU and set a school record for most time played. LSU had to substitute for him because of injury only once in four years. In 1947, Y.A. tackled a Vanderbilt runner head on and was knocked out. After Tittle spent several minutes on the sidelines sniffing ammonia, the team doctor said he couldn't return to the game.

"Why?" hollered line coach Swanson.

"The boy's hardly breathing."

"You're a doctor. *Make him breathe*," Swanson screamed.

Before the physician could reply, Y.A., concerned more with Swanson's ire than the doctor's warning, jumped up, ran back into the game and connected on five straight passes.

He set another record. During his senior year, LSU played the University of Mississippi, then led by Charlie Conerly. With Ole Miss in front, 20–18, Y.A. intercepted a pass thrown by Conerly's replacement near LSU's 40. The intended receiver made a grab for Y.A. but only pulled off the belt that held up Y.A.'s pants.

Y.A. started chugging toward the Ole Miss end zone, ball in one hand, pants clutched in the other. At the 20, two defenders closed in on him. Y.A. shifted the ball from his right hand to his left so he could use his right to push them off. He forgot about his pants. Down they went—taking Y.A. with them. Watching, 40,000 howling spectators and Minnette De-Loach, of Marshall, Texas, Y.A.'s fiancée.

Cleveland of the new All-American Conference signed Tittle but immediately sent him to try to save a sinking Baltimore franchise. Y.A. was Rookie of the Year in 1948 in the All-America Conference (as was Charlie Conerly with the Giants in the NFL that season). Baltimore collapsed after 1950. The players were thrown into the college draft. Kyle Rote, a bonus pick, was taken first by the Giants. Tittle was the third man selected, by San Francisco.

Y.A. walked into a difficult situation when he joined the Giants. Charlie Conerly was the quarterback and no one from the tightly knit offensive unit was going to become friendly with the man who might take his job. The defensive team, which was just as close, also went its own way and, typical of many great Giant teams, didn't want much to do with any of the offensive "pretty boys," much less an old, bald quarterback. With relatively few exceptions, the entire squad had been together at least since 1956.

Tittle was assigned to room with backfield coach Heinrich who would help him learn the Giant offense. Although Y.A. was older than Heinrich, players don't go out with coaches and Y.A. was left alone while the team went off after daily practice to the local friendly tavern. Like the new boy on the block, he kept his room door closed so no one would see him sitting alone.

When the Giants traveled to Los Angeles for an exhibition game against the Rams, Y.A. went down early to the hotel lobby, hoping for a spontaneous dinner invitation from the players passing through. Finally, he asked the doorman if he knew where the players had gone to eat. Then he walked to that restaurant and pretended he was looking for a nonexistent friend. Several Giants finally asked him to sit with them "while he waited."

During Tittle's first play the following night against the Rams, he bobbled the handoff and fell on the ball. A half ton of Rams fell on him—and cracked several bones in his back. Out for five weeks.

While he suffered, more from embarrassment and the return of nagging self-doubt than pain, Y.A. found himself beginning to root silently for Charlie. "I used to sit on the bench in San Francisco with Frankie Albert and, later, Brodie playing and clapping with my fingers crossed," he said, "hoping the SOB's next pass is intercepted because that was the only way I was going to get into the game.

"I couldn't do that with Charlie. He had so much class that although it was surely gnawing on his pride to see me there, he could come over in practice when I did something well and say, 'Well, you're looking pretty good, Y.A.'

"I knew what it was like to have someone else come in to play your position," Y.A. said. "We were both in the twilight of our careers." Y.A. broke off abruptly at this point, and I realized from his expression how strong an impact those events now 15 years old had had on him. For the first time, I understood with heightened clarity how painful that time had been for both Y.A. and Charlie. I would have been happy just sharing the work with Charlie. But when I got the starter's job, I knew how it must have hurt.

"Charlie was tough. He could cope, could handle physical punishment *and* mental punishment without letting either get to him. There was an extraordinary dignity about that man."

Sherman handled the situation well. He spoke with Charlie and Y.A. "Any split between you two old guys will crack this club right down the middle," he said. "It isn't going to be easy for any of us. Barring injury, there never will be a time when one of you isn't playing. You are both number one, no matter who starts."

"I was surprised when I came to the Giants," Y.A. told me. "The players didn't seem to have the physical ability of the men I had left behind on the 49ers. But they were far more successful. One reason was maturity. Their age and experience made them virtually unbeatable."

There was a second reason: The Giants *expected* to win. We based our end of season plans around the championship game. The 49ers hoped to win; the Giants expected to.

"I had never seen the spirit that club had," Y.A. said, "both the offensive and the defensive players. The defense dubbed themselves, the DVW's, Defense vs. The World, and they were thoroughly confident they could handle any team."

Before the season began, the Giants traded for 26-year-old Del Shofner, a combination end and defensive back at Los Angeles, and tight end Joe Walton. The Shofner trade was a management error of major magnitude on the part of the Rams. They'd given up on one of the finest athletes I've ever seen because of a few nagging injuries that had bothered Del the previous season. Shofner could leave almost any defensive back in the league and instantly became Y.A.'s primary receiver. He broke my record for single-season receptions during his first year with the Giants; he caught 68 passes for 11 touchdowns. Del was the best end Y.A. had ever played with. Tittle had Billy Wilson in San Francisco. Billy had an extraordinary pair of hands, but he wasn't fast. Shofner had both the hands and the great speed.

Y.A. opened the 1961 season watching from the bench. Charlie started against St. Louis but the Giants did little offensively or defensively and lost, 21–10. New York was leading Pittsburgh in the second game, 10–7, when Conerly was shaken up. Tittle made his first appearance as a Giant. He hit his first six passes in succession and ended the day with 10 completions in 12 attempts. The Giants won, 17–14.

Feelings erupted only once. Early in the third game, against Washington, the Giants fell behind when one of Charlie's receivers missed his pass route and the pass was intercepted and run back for a touchdown. Tittle had been warming up on the sideline and Sherman chose that moment to send him in.

Charlie slammed the helmet to the ground, walked to the far end of the bench and sat down. Y.A. finished the game, bringing New York from behind in the last quarter to win, 24–21. Following the game, reporters in the locker room quizzed Tittle, Conerly and Sherman. All of them characteristically refused to comment on a situation that could have destroyed the ball club.

Y.A. started most of the games that followed but he needed help from Charlie twice, against Los Angeles and in the second game against Philadelphia, the defending league champion. The Washington game at midseason was the turning point. It followed a one-point loss to Dallas. I never saw the Giants play that year because I was always scouting their next week's opponent. I had felt Washington's new cornerbacks were vulnerable to deep passes, particularly since New York finally had a deep threat in Shofner.

The weapon was simple. The results were explosive. New York used a three-receiver pattern with Kyle and Joe Walton, the ends, breaking downfield just a few yards and then turning in to pull coverage from Washington's two deep men. Shofner, set as a flanker to the left, ran a "fly," a straight, all-out sprint. The Redskins made an early mistake, single coverage on Shofner. Del got behind a cornerback, took Tittle's pass on the 10 and scored untouched. Tittle threw three touchdown passes as New York won, 53–0. The Giants went on to win four and tie one of the seven remaining games (scoring 170 points) to win the eastern division title.

Part of the credit for the first win over Philadelphia, which put the Giants in a tie for first place, went to Pete Previte, popular clubhouse man for the football Giants and baseball

Yankees. He was forever making suggestions that we laughingly accepted in the locker room and forgot about on the field. But Pete was very knowledgeable about baseball and in this instance that knowledge paid off. "In baseball, fast men are put into the line-up in scoring situations," he reasoned, "why not football?"

He suggested using defensive backs Erich Barnes and Jim Patton, both of whom could run the 100 in under 10 seconds. The play worked well in practice so it was put into the Philadelphia ready list. With seconds remaining in the first half, Barnes and Patton replaced running backs Alex Webster and Bob Gaiters. Tittle shocked the Eagles' secondary with five receivers—Rote, Shofner and Walton were the additional three—and hit Barnes, who had beaten his man by a step, on the Eagle 26 for a 62-yard touchdown play. That put New York ahead to stay.

"Charlie pulling out the second Philadelphia game brought us into the final game against Cleveland needing only a tie, which we got, to take the eastern championship," Y.A. said. "He won two big games coming off the bench. That's the toughest way to win them. You're cold. You don't have the feel of the game. It takes time to gauge the speed of your receivers, the wind and the condition of the field. The defense knows you're cold and they come at you like all hell. It's like pinch-hitting with two out in the ninth. The pressure is immense."

Charlie *was* hurting inside. Unless injured, he hadn't sat on a football bench since junior high school. Yet he was quick to compliment Tittle and do it sincerely.

After the first Pittsburgh win: "Y.A. made three or four big calls on third-down plays," Charlie told one writer. "Sometimes a quarterback can call a play that isn't worth a damn, but Y.A. didn't waste a single third-down situation."

After the second Pittsburgh game: "He was the master all the time he was out there." For our silent Mississippian, those are speeches, believe me; and far more than I had ever heard him say to a writer about himself.

For Y.A., 1961 and the eastern division title "was just like being born again."

In August, Tittle had had no one to have dinner with in Los Angeles. Four months later, the Giants gathered in Jim Downey's restaurant in New York to celebrate the winning of the eastern championship. And when all the scheduled speeches and tributes were done, a spontaneous clamor went up around the room: "Y.A., Y.A., Y.A." and the same bald man with jug ears slowly stood and talked about "the greatest year in my life."

By midseason 1961, the shotgun was dead in San Francisco as defenses adjusted to it and Y.A. was the liveliest thing in the National Football League. Instead of a premature retirement and a lifetime wondering, "Could I or couldn't I?", he had become the center of everything a championship in New York offered.

Y.A. was a flaming spirit and he captured New York within months, well before the 1961 season was over. He was given a day—and a yacht—on the last game of his first year. He began making commercials, giving product testimonials, appearing on television and magazine covers.

"There is no other place to be a winner," he said, "and Minnette and I were just country people pinching ourselves the whole time we were there." Y.A. liked to play that country boy role just a bit. I always had the feeling that he was smiling inside at us every time he did.

Y.A.'s highly emotional, always charged-up method of playing captivated the city for three incredible years of a four-year stay. For a time he turned New York into as close as a big city could get to the kind of community Green Bay became during Vince Lombardi's years there.

Tittle, the place and the time meshed. "Dee-fense" already had become part of the vocabulary. With Y.A. came "the bomb" for the long, beautiful passes he loved so much. His playing tenure concluded the 10 best years in Giant history. Even his "downfall"—and it wasn't *his* as far as I was concerned—fit because it was kind of a bittersweet end to three storybook years no one had expected.

Pro football, television, advertisers, and a mushrooming sports public met during the '58 through '60 period. The Giants and Y.A. were there to pick the first ripe fruit.

People saw themselves in Y.A.: the agony as game after game got down to the closing minutes before Y.A. pulled them out and, sometimes, failed; the way he had been cast off; his baldness; his ungainliness; his frustration when a play went badly, and he drop-kicked his helmet 20 feet in front of 62,000 people in Yankee Stadium; his running down the sideline when the Giant defensive unit intercepted a pass, and almost getting garroted in his excitement because he forgot to remove the telephone headset connecting him with the spotter coach on the top of the stadium; his bootlegging 21 yards for a touchdown, gleefully tossing the ball high in the air, skipping a few steps, tripping, falling, yet getting up with a huge grin as if to say, "Old Y.A. put one over on you again, world"; his idiosyncracies. (Tittle, prematurely bald, was so sensitive that he rarely uncovered, even on the bench. When he was traded to the Giants, a wire-service photographer came to his house. Tittle was packing so the photographer asked if he could get a shot of that. Although pantless, Tittle put on a fedora and told the photographer to go ahead.)

Y.A. wasn't perfect—so everyone loved him.

And Y.A. kept the fun going:

"Ah enjoy calling plays myself, especially when we're going good, but that's when Shofner comes back to the huddle and he's got a pass he wants to call. Rosey Brown comes back and says he's got his man licked, Gaiters wants another try and Sherman has to keep his hand in.

"But when we get down there on the five-yard line, fourth down and still five, Shofner's got his head down studying the design of his shoes, Brown's looking the other way, Gaiters is at the far end of the huddle, Sherman is talking to some other coach and that's when I get to call a play."

The big-eared, big-nosed asthmatic who stuttered like a teenager when excited was a born leader. He radiated so much confidence that the Giants in those years were shocked when he—and they—didn't win.

His confidence sometimes got him into trouble. Y.A. insisted on running with the ball.

"I loved bootlegging. (The quarterback fakes a handoff, hides the ball behind his hip and circles the end, a solitary figure running away from the flow of the action.) I fool everybody. I'm running full speed, but going so slow everyone says, 'Oh, he couldn't *possibly* have the ball.' "

Most of Tittle's injuries came when he kept the ball and ran. His cheekbone was shattered one day early in his career when he bootlegged for a touchdown against Detroit. A back grabbed his arm, Y.A. fell and rolled into the end zone as a safety dived to stop him and smashed his knee into Tittle's face. He suffered a concussion running into the end zone against Detroit with the Giants in 1962. His face was badly cut that same year when he ran against Pittsburgh. He suffered back injuries with the bootleg against Green Bay and Dallas.

"I had learned a lot watching Frankie Albert play in San Francisco," Y.A. said. "I *had* a lot to learn. I was still shy; I was still hesitant about taking charge. Albert threw passes with a "floppy" left arm—if he ever threw a spiral he'd have a heart attack—but he was an outstanding quarterback. He was quick, he was glib, he brought something to football that I had never thought about before. He came to the huddle and he had bounce. He was a fun maker.

"I watched Albert bootleg and I realized that it was not meant necessarily to gain yards, but to give a lift to the club.

It was a touch of something that was a little off-beat. When I watched that little short quarterback hide the ball on his hip and make 15 yards and then run out of bounds, it was as if he were saying to the other team, 'I've got ya; right in the palm of my hand. I can do anything I want to do with you guys.'

"He was right. That's when I started to bootleg. I never ran the bootleg unless I was pretty sure it would go. You're faking handing the ball off and soon everyone's running one way, offense, defense, and the only one going the other way is this old bald guy and people think, 'God, what is he *doing*?' and you run out of bounds after a 15-yard gain and come back to the huddle and your players say, 'You dumb son of a bitch, you're gonna get killed out there.' It's a turn-onner.

"I was an orthodox quarterback before Albert. Then I learned some of the things that ignite your players, yourself, the fans. That's why I risked it, even though it was dangerous; it was worth it for the rewards the team would get out of it.

"Albert used to make up plays in the huddle when we had a safe lead, for fun. He'd call on our huge 270-pound tackle Leo Nomellini—who wanted to be a fullback—to come into the backfield and run into the line. He'd get nowhere but again Albert was 'telling' the other team, 'I can play with you.'

"Frank was a great leader. He brought the players into the game and that was so important. He wasn't a strategist, worrying about who should block whom, and the best way to stop blitzing linebackers. He was an organized sandlotter and that's what the game of football is. If a quarterback can keep the club moving, he's better than all the 'brains' in the world.

"Football is for fun. I never played a game in my life that I didn't enjoy. I loved to go to practice right up to the very end. That's why it was so hard to retire. I never quit liking it.

"We worked like hell to prepare for each game. But there was always room for fun."

Y.A. often went after his own players if he didn't like the

way they worked. Against Dallas in 1961, rookie halfback Bob Gaiters took a handoff from Tittle, danced for a couple of steps while his hole opened and closed and was dumped for a loss. Tittle didn't even wait for Gaiters to get up. He knelt beside Gaiters, pounded the ground with his fist and screamed, "That's the last time you do that. Next time, bust in there." The astonished rookie could only mutter: "Yes, sir."

Against Pittsburgh the same year, Gaiters swept around end, saw Big Daddy Lipscomb, 285 pounds and one of the best defensive tackles in the history of pro football, leading the defenders coming at him and stepped outside to avoid being tackled. Tittle was there in an instant: "Don't you ever do that when I'm around. Put your head down and go."

During the same game, Tittle bootlegged around end, was shoved out of bounds and Lipscomb went after him and knocked him down. The Giants' Jim Katcavage went off the bench after Lipscomb but was pulled back. Tittle returned to the game with blood streaming from a cut over the eye, courtesy of Lipscomb.

In the second quarter, Y.A. ran again and, again, was shoved out of bounds and behind the players' bench when Lou Michaels, 235 pounds, leaped the bench and knocked Tittle down. Y.A. was shaken but responded by throwing an immediate pass to Alex Webster that put the Giants in front, 21–7.

Lipscomb and Michaels pounded Tittle so hard in that game that when Lipscomb came to the Giants' locker room after the game to congratulate the team, his good friend, Rosey Brown, stared coldly at him and said, "Big Daddy, sometimes I got to wonder about you."

Y.A. became sort of a captain-father confessor to our team. However it didn't always work. New York's first draft choice in 1964 was a running back named Joe Don Looney. He had the potential to be an extraordinary player. But—there were problems.

He injured his leg early in training camp. So Sherman told him to see the trainer about it. To Allie's amazement, Looney refused.

His reason? "It's my leg. I know more about it than the trainer."

He wouldn't go to Detroit for an exhibition game. "I can't play: why should I go?" he asked me.

"You're part of the team," I said.

"I'm not part of the team if I can't play," he replied.

Joe Don came in an hour after curfew one night and was fined. "Not fair," he said, "I was in bed an hour early last night, so we should be even up."

He wouldn't throw his used socks into a marked bin because "I'm not going to do what any sign tells me to do."

Although I didn't see it, I understand that in scrimmages, he often ran one way when the play called for him to go another. His reason: "Anybody can run where the blockers are. A good football player makes his own holes."

As a last-ditch measure, Wellington Mara and Allie Sherman asked Y.A. and me to try to talk to the young man. Joe Don was 6'1", 224 pounds and ran the 100 in something like 9.7. They wanted to keep him.

We were still in training camp at Fairfield (Conn.) University. Joe Don was lying down in his room listening to music when we found him.

Y.A. flopped on the other bed and started to tell Joe Don about his trade to New York from San Francisco, which somehow Y.A. equated with Looney's problems: how difficult it was leaving the team where he had spent most of his career, his family, his business, being traded for a rookie lineman, coming to a team in a strange city with a popular quarterback ahead of him and how "alone" Y.A. had felt.

Clearly talking from his heart and, perhaps for the first time outside of his family discussing his gut feelings about the trade, Tittle went on for about 20 minutes with Joe Don and me listening intently.

Finally, Y.A. finished and stopped, serious, sad, thinking of what had happened just three years earlier.

Joe Don broke an embarrassing silence. He sat up, completely caught up in Tittle's reverie, and said sympathetically, "It must have been *really* tough, Y.A. Anything I can do for you?"

Joe Don didn't last much longer with New York and moved through a couple of teams. He paused briefly with the Detroit Lions. In a scene reminiscent of Y.A.'s "from the heart" advice, the Lions asked Joe Schmidt, the great middle linebacker, to see why Joe Don hadn't come to practice one day.

Schmidt walked into Joe Don's room and there was our errant ballplayer listening to music.

"Joe," Schmidt said, "we missed you at practice."

"I'm glad you did, Joe."

"You know, I've been with this club 12 years and I've never missed or been late to a practice. In all that time."

Looney blinked. "You never missed one practice in 12 years?"

"That's right."

"Boy, Joe, pull up a chair. If there was ever someone who needed a day off, it's you."

During the offseason after 1961, I decided I wanted to play again. Doctors had told me to quit after the Eagle game late in the 1960 season. They were afraid that the "deep concussion" I had sustained in that game might lead to further injury.

I followed their advice and the advice of friends and re-

tired a bit too quickly. I considered 1961 a wasted year because I didn't play. I knew I could still play. I had kept in
good condition playing basketball two or three times a week
and working out with the Giants. I ran dummy scrimmages
and pass patterns with them. I knew I could beat half the guys
they had there.

I liked the life. I liked the people. I was doing well in broad-
casting, probably making more money than I could with the
Giants. I knew that was ultimately what I wanted to do, but
I could do that later. I couldn't always play football.

Wellington Mara and Sherman agreed. A neurologist examined me and found no problems. So I gave notice to CBS
and when they found someone to take my shows, I quit, went
back to California and began working out twice a day.

At training camp for the 1962 season, Alex Webster and
Phil King were the running backs and Sherman moved me to
flanker to take the spot Kyle had played until he retired
after 1961. I hurt my back in the first week of training camp
and didn't have a chance to work with Y.A. until the final exhibition game against Philadelphia. I didn't play well. My
timing was off and I dropped at least four passes.

I sat out the first two games of the season. My back still
hurt. Aaron Thomas was playing flanker. I was depressed and
seriously thinking of quitting; perhaps my return wasn't such
a good idea.

Then Thomas hurt his knee and I started the third game
against the Steelers. Tittle threw four touchdown passes. I
caught one of them and three others that helped set up the
remaining scores.

From that point, I was back. I caught 10 touchdown passes
during the season, two less than Shofner who again led the
Giants in touchdown receptions. Balancing Shofner, King,
Webster, Walton and me, Tittle kept the opposition off
balance. With Charlie Conerly retired, Y.A., in his second

year with the Giants, had emerged as the team's absolute leader.

He knew the abilities and limitations of all his offensive teammates, but he had an uncanny telepathy with his receivers. He wanted his pass patterns run precisely the way they were supposed to be run: so many steps upfield, fake, cut, so many steps inside or outside. We practiced for hours until he probably could have thrown his passes blindfolded.

He and I shared a rhythm. He would turn from the center and run back, not back-pedal, always the same number of steps, plant the back foot and throw. He released the ball most of the time before I made my last cut and it was always in the right place at the precise instant. If I had only a half-step lead on my defender, that was all I needed.

Y.A. did it the same way every time. After about a half-hour of practicing, we'd have to move to a new place on the field because he'd have literally dug a hole with his rear foot at precisely seven and a half yards.

While Shofner was Y.A.'s deep man, I became his short man. Our favorite pattern was a zigout (the name coming from the z-like path). My assignment was to drive on the cornerback, move hard to the inside and look back at Tittle. He pumped a fake, forcing the cornerback to commit to the inside just as I planted my inside foot and broke hard to the outside. The pattern required absolute precision, a kind of oneness. It became the Giants' most effective call on third and long.

Y.A. was fun to play with and watch. He loved excitement. He wouldn't peck, peck, peck at the other teams with short yardage plays. He loved to score big and long. We'd go out there and score 17 points so fast the team we were playing didn't know what happened.

We won 12 of 14 games in 1962. Tittle tied a league record by throwing seven touchdown passes in one game

against Washington. We clinched the conference title with two
games still to play.

After the last game of the season, Y.A. was dancing around
the locker room with a Coke in his hand and singing: "We
won it. We won it again. This is Christmas. It's heaven for the
second time." He was marvelous. The oldest man on the
team kept the rest of us young.

(Y.A. wrote a letter to Wellington Mara after that season.
It took him three months to get it right. He wanted to be
the first football pro to earn $100,000 a year and, in his letter,
he justified his reasoning. Wellington didn't argue, just said
he'd come out to California and talk with Y.A. Tittle's friends,
told him not to fraternize with Wellington, to be tough, have
him come by Y.A.'s office when Y.A. had time to see him. But
that just wasn't Y.A. He picked Wellington up at the airport
and brought him home. Wellington stayed three days in
Y.A.'s house and they had a great time. Y.A. didn't get the
$100,000.)

The 1963 season was tougher. Y.A. led the Giants to a
division title for the third consecutive year. But we didn't
win the championship until the last day of the season.

Tittle, 36 years old, cavorted like a kid through every
game. In the opener against Baltimore—our first victory over
that club since Johnny Unitas had become its quarterback—
Y.A. threw for three touchdowns and waddled for one more.
He bootlegged it from the nine, saw two linebackers coming
up to get him and our nut, the quarterback, thought he was a
fullback. He put his head down and dove into them and the
end zone. He scored, but at the price of a partially collapsed
lung. He sat out the next game; we lost to Pittsburgh, 31–0.
It was the first time in 10 years the Giants hadn't scored in
a game.

Although most quarterbacks would have been sidelined for
several weeks, Y.A. was back the next week to complete 15 of

25 passes to crush Philadelphia, 37–14. We lost two games the rest of the season with Tittle playing, one to St. Louis on a late Cardinal score after we had fumbled and the other to Cleveland when Jimmy Brown put on a one-man show. Two weeks later, Tittle completed 20 passes to whip the Browns, 33–6.

Y.A., who led what was to become the second highest scoring team in the history of the league that season and who would again be elected the NFL's Most Valuable Player, was amazing and consistent, Sunday after Sunday.

He wasn't supposed to play in the first game against the Cardinals because he had been out during the week with a severe viral infection. He connected with 17 of 28 passes as we won, 38–21. (He wasn't too ill to stick the needle into me, either. During the second quarter, he threw a pass from the St. Louis 41 into the end zone. I had to leap for it, caught the end of the ball, flipped it up and as I hit the ground turned over enough to catch it. Tittle didn't say a word until the game was over; then as he walked by my locker said, to no one in particular, "If that had been Shofner, he would have caught it coming back." Y.A. was never impressed by my speed.)

St. Louis, Cleveland, Pittsburgh, and New York fought for the division title until the last two weeks. The Steelers, playing us on the last day, needed only a tie for its first championship but we won, 33–17.

Paul Brown, the Cleveland coach, said Y.A. was the "best passer in football" that year and most everyone agreed. After we scored the first seven times that we had the ball against Cleveland, a writer called Tittle "astonishing (because) he is so good Sunday after Sunday." When we defeated the Cardinals, St. Louis coach Wally Lemm said "We're probably seeing the best year any quarterback has ever had."

Against the Eagles, Tittle completed 13 of 15 during the first half. Nick Skorich, Philadelphia coach, said afterward,

"He's the best in the game today and no one—a Van Brocklin, a Graham, a Baugh, I don't care who—ever had a better season than he's having."

They were all right.

Before the 1962 and 1963 league-title games, Y.A. and our team were the focus of extraordinary attention. Fans at a hockey game in Madison Square Garden began to chant between periods, "Beat Green Bay (the 1962 opponent) . . . beat Green Bay." Disc jockeys and store owners in Manhattan picked up the line. Strangers stopped Y.A. on the street or in restaurants and cheered him on as they would an old friend.

It multiplied in 1963 when we were preparing for Chicago and the NFL championship. I was moonlighting on local television and I interviewed Y.A. a week before the game. Everyone looking in learned that he lived in Eastchester, a suburb of New York City. Y.A. didn't have an unlisted number so his phone rang until game time. Boys and girls knocked on his door daily to pledge their support.

He found a ticket for overtime parking on his car. Written across the back: "Forget the ticket, Y.A. Murder the Bears." A Christmas package was delivered with "Beat the Bears, Y.A." written on one side in crayon by the men in the local post office. The teaching sisters in the parochial school Y.A.'s boys were attending sent word that they were saying the rosary for Y.A. every day until the game. And the Tittles weren't even Catholics.

"A lot of people were rooting for me, I guess, because they kind of figured I was getting close to the end of my career and that I would not have many more chances," he said. "I think all the people who were in their middle or late thirties were on our side. Not all of them were Giant fans. But this was an older ball club with a lot of guys who had been around for a long time. We were symbols to people in that age group for reasons I'm sure were not even related to football."

We should have beaten the Packers in 1962 and the Bears in 1963 for the league titles.

(I'll take Y.A.'s word for the 1961 championship game. I wasn't there. "We were hopelessly outclassed by the Packers. It was in Green Bay, the temperature as I recall was under 5°, there was a blizzard and we couldn't adjust. We were down about 37–0 with a minute or so left to go and I kept wanting to throw, to try to get something on the scoreboard while the guys in the huddle were thinking only of a hot shower and glared at me everytime I called a pass. They wanted runs up the middle, nothing that would stop the clock.")

In 1962, we had gale force winds and a temperature at about 9°. I was there for this one, at the end of my comeback year, and wished I hadn't been. Packer coach Vince Lombardi must have ordered the weather that day directly from Pope John. You can throw in rain; you can throw in snow; but you can't throw in gusty, high wind. I didn't get a pass all day. Y.A. threw one to me that went almost straight up in the air. He threw balls that landed behind him. It was quite simple. The Packers were a running team. We were a passing team. We lost, 16–7.

The following year, we knew we were better than the Bears. We had a great offensive team and a good defensive team. We reached the Chicago 14 on our first series of plays in the game. I knew I could beat defensive back Bennie McRae on our favorite zig-out pass to the corner. I told Y.A. and we scored our touchdown.

But just as Y.A. released the ball, Chicago linebacker Larry Morris hit him across the left leg. The knee started to stiffen. Late in the second period, Chicago intercepted a pass and took it 61 yards for the tying score. Don Chandler kicked a field goal and we led, 10–7. Then Morris dove again into Tittle's left knee. "It was as if a knife had been stuck into the knee joint," Y.A. said. "The pain shot clear up my leg."

Before the second half started, Sherman asked Tittle if he thought he could play. The decision was Y.A.'s to make.

"I didn't know what to say," Y.A. told a writer years later. "Injuries are funny things. Football is an emotional game and sometimes you can do amazing things when you're hurt. I remember once I went into a game with two sprained ankles. I could barely walk into the huddle. But once I got under that center, I was cured on the spot. In 1953, I played a game with a shattered cheekbone and completed 29 passes. I went in for San Francisco once with a broken hand and won the game.

"I pulled a hamstring muscle with San Francisco in 1957 and was supposed to be out for three weeks, but John Brodie went bad in the first half the next week against Green Bay and Hickey asked, 'Can you play, Tittle?' What does a ballplayer say in a spot like that? I tried. I got out there and threw a couple of touchdown passes and we won, 27–20."

For anyone who still had to know, the Bear game in 1963 was another one that proved Tittle's guts. He had no business playing the second half. His only backup was rookie Glynn Griffing. So Y.A. came in with his knee shot full of Novocaine and heavily taped. It was clear to all of us that he was playing in extreme pain. Yet he never complained about a missed assignment, a dropped ball or a knee that in spite of the pain killer must have felt as if it was held together by ligaments turned to spaghetti. Tittle was unable to set up to throw well. He couldn't drop straight back to pass. He had to back-pedal, which is far slower. He couldn't maneuver. The Bears' defensive coach George Allen knew this and Chicago kept coming at Y.A. with everyone but the ticket takers.

Another pass was intercepted and run back for a touchdown. That's how they won, 14–10, on two passes intercepted after Y.A. was put out of commission early in the first quarter.

Y.A. was on crutches for two weeks, but he still was criticized because New York lost. Many guys I played with and many I know today wouldn't have gone back into that game with a gun.

1964. The team that had won three straight division championships fell to last place as an attempt to replace older players overnight failed.

Sam Huff, Dick Modzelewski, Phil King and Joe Walton were traded before the season began. Del Shofner and several other key players were hurt and missed most of the year. New York won two games.

Y.A. was hurt badly during the second game. Steeler end John Baker caught him blindside trying to get off a screen pass. Y.A. had no chance. As he fell under the 270-pound Baker, his rib cartilage went, his helmet was knocked off and he received a gash on his forehead. A photograph taken at that moment, with Y.A. on his knees, bald head exposed, bleeding, gasping for breath, stunned, told the story of the 1964 season.

Two days after the Pittsburgh injury, Y.A. was throwing passes in practice with his ribs taped up, insisting he was ready to play.

"I shouldn't have played for three weeks, as the doctors ordered," Y.A. said. "I foolishly went back too soon. That was the most painful injury I'd ever had. Every time I was knocked down, I couldn't get up. I literally couldn't stand. Somebody would have to help me to the sideline and after four or five plays the pain would lessen and I'd go back.

"If I had stayed out and come back well, I might have helped the team instead of adding to its physical and psychological distress. You can't go up to a sportswriter and say, 'Hey, look, I'm hurt. Please don't say the team is finished.'"

Y.A.—who had thrown a record 36 touchdown passes in 1963, four in the last game December 27—didn't fall apart in the seven months between the two seasons. The team fell apart around him.

But fans turned against Tittle. When we were waiting on the field for the last game of the season, Y.A. looked up at the December sky and said, "No one could ever understand what it feels like to stand here and get ready for a game in Yankee Stadium." He could still feel the excitement of the prior three years. But the crowd apparently could not. He was introduced—and booed.

It was figuratively just one step from Y.A.'s injury against Pittsburgh in the second game to his last game of the season. He played only the first half as the Giants were clubbed by Cleveland, 52–20. On the last play of a 27–year career, Y.A. was helped up from the mud by his old buddy, Dick Modzelewski, now working for the other side. "Little Mo," a gentle guy for all his aggressiveness on the field, helped Y.A. brush some of the muck off, but he couldn't find anything to say to him.

He came as a backup, a substitute, a 35-year-old man coming to "help" one who was five years older. The substitute became number one and remained for three years. No quarterback in the history of the NFL before or since ever had three consecutive years like that. Ignore his passing and ignore his exuberance and ignore the league championships that were lost each year. Y.A. moved the Giants three times to conference titles in extraordinary ways.

When I visited Y.A. recently in his home in suburban San Francisco, we talked about the last day. We had been sitting together on the bench during the fourth quarter of that awful game and I had told Y.A. he should consider staying on in pro ball and ask to be traded to another team. He was finished with the Giants. They were putting a new team together.

But I knew several clubs wanted him. And, probably, he

could have picked up exactly where he was in 1963 because he wasn't hurt. He was 38 but healthy. Charlie Conerly had been voted Most Valuable Player at 38. (Five years later, Y.A. came back as Giant quarterback coach and he and I put on shorts and shoes and ran pass patterns and that ball zipped just as true and fast as it always had.)

"I didn't ask to be traded because I didn't think I could ever top the first three years with New York," Y.A. said slowly. "It was great and I didn't want to become mediocre. Pride? Fear? I don't think I could have done what Johnny Unitas, perhaps the best quarterback the game has ever seen, did when he went to San Diego after his career in Baltimore."

Y.A. is the same incurable romantic now as he was when he played. We talked then about the Giants—as veterans of any common experience would talk. Y.A. quickly drifted back 12 years.

"Put yourself with me. Every year you were struggling and saying the next year was gonna do it, was gonna be the year— and then all of a sudden, the unbelievable dreams do come true. You're in the great years in The House That Ruth Built in front of 62,000 people and Ed Sullivan orders his dancers to devise a Tittle polka for the show and you're being called to endorse products, make commercials, and most important, play winning ball and then"—he snapped his fingers—"you're 38 and the door closes. No more."

Y.A. drifted off. He wasn't talking to me any longer. "You know, for 27 years, every time the center gave me the ball, I chuckled. By God, I thought, I've got hold of it again.

"I have a fine family. My business has treated us well. I play tennis and I'm a good tennis player. I have a boat and I like to use it. I don't drink. I don't smoke. My health is good. But these last eight to 10 years. . . .

"I'm like Peter Pan. I keep thinking the ball game will start again.

"But it won't."

Dan
Gable

M inneapolis. Weigh-in time for a match between an American wresting team and a group of Russians, acknowledged to be the world's best wrestlers. An announcement is made that Dan Gable has hurt his knee and can't participate. The Russian who was to be his opponent turns and races down to his team's locker room shouting in glee: "No Gable, no Gable."

Sofia, Bulgaria. The 1971 World Championships. Gable is wrestling in the semifinals against Japan's best man. Midway through the second of three periods, Gable's opponent collapses under the American's attack. He falls back exhausted and lies on the mat. He doesn't have the strength to continue.

Tiflis, USSR. A dual meet between the United States and Russia. Russia sweeps every class except 150 pounds. There, Gable wins his 10th consecutive match over a Russian. That night, the Russian team manager announces a country-wide search for someone who can beat Gable in the 1972 Olympics.

Munich, Germany. The Olympics. Gable wins a gold medal in the 149½-pound division. It's the first time in the history of the Olympics an American wrestler has won without giving up a point to six opponents. He also pinned three of the six, the equivalent of a knockout in boxing. He accomplished this after his eyelid was gashed severely in his first match. He had to win fast or face possible injury disqualification.

The subject of all this: A mild-looking, reserved 27-year-old Iowan, idol to a nation of schoolboys and the most exciting wrestler this country has ever seen.

What is courage? A brave act at the risk of one's life? Superhuman effort for a moment in the face of danger? We sometimes read or hear or see such impressive deeds. But I think courage has many faces. Dan Gable's single-minded assault on a dream set as a teenager is, to me, heroic. To dedicate one's mind, body and heart to an almost unreachable goal every day of every year from early adolescence through high school, college, and two years further requires an extraordinary intensity of purpose and discipline. To push one's body to the limit of endurance and then beyond, to deny oneself normal pleasures while all around are enjoying those pleasures, to persevere under grueling competition is, to me, a rare facet of courage. Dan Gable's courage.

I know of no sport where a champion hasn't begun with talent and then concentrated on honing it. Gable is perhaps the lone exception. His natural abilities are minimal. All he had was a desire to be the world's best wrestler.

Gable shut out the world from 1966 to 1972 when he won his gold medal in the Olympics. He literally eliminated everything else in his life that might interfere. His motivation? It may have been the example of his parents, both of whom are extremely hardworking. It may have been the murder of Dan's high-school-age sister when the rest of the family were away on a fishing trip; Dan said his wrestling "would be for Diane." It may, simply, have been a way for a once extremely shy, average-sized midwestern boy, to find a place for himself in the world.

Late summer, 1966. Gable was about to become a freshman at Iowa State, a national collegiate wrestling power. A friend, Bob Buzzard, finished his factory shift at 7:00 P.M.

and came directly to the Gable house to work out with Dan. Buzzard was then in graduate school. He had won two Big Eight wrestling titles. They had practiced together all summer.

"Dan was a tough kid," Buzzard said. "Some days, I'd crunch him. Some days, I'd fool around and let him make some moves. But on this last day before I went back to Eastern Michigan University, I wanted to show him he had a ways to go even though he had won three consecutive state high school championships."

When the stronger, more experienced Buzzard finished that evening with Dan, the 17-year-old fell down on the mat and began to cry—tears of anger.

"Right then," Gable told me years later, "I knew how far I had to go. I vowed I wouldn't *ever* let anyone destroy me again. I was going to work at it every day, so hard that I would be the toughest guy in the world."

Large aspiration for a 17-year-old. Except Gable never forgot it. Vince Lombardi said that fatigue makes cowards of us all. Gable decided that, impossible as it sounds, he would never allow himself to get tired in a match again. He would never again fail for lack of stamina and endurance.

That was the start of his wrestling strategy: wear them down. Wrestling is a game of offense and defense, like most sports. Dan's strength and endurance allowed him to be on the offense all the time—always attacking, always pressing, never giving an opponent a chance to relax or to counterattack.

Dan was always virtually as fresh at the end of a contest as at the beginning. Most wrestlers, including the best in international competition, take certain positions during a match to catch their breath, to rest a moment from nine minutes of wrestling. Gable never did.

He won most of his matches in the middle of the second period. Until then, a match usually was close; Dan sometimes was trailing. But his opponent's strength drained under

Gable's pressure. In one typical match, he was ahead, 3–2, with four minutes gone; at four minutes and *50 seconds,* Dan was leading, 16–2.

Most of the wrestlers Gable competed with throughout his career had far more natural ability than he.

Gable had started from scratch in high school. He worked for everything a champion wrestler must have—strength, stamina, technique, balance ("There were days I must have jumped rope a thousand times"), coordination, agility.

Gable remembered his teenage pledge. He did work out every day for the next six years.

I recall watching Dan on his exercise bicycle in his basement. As he pumped, he kept turning the device that made the pedals harder to push. When he got to the point where he said his legs "died," he made the pedals even harder to work and did another 15 minutes.

He worked out on the wrestling mat at least once every day, usually two or three times. He didn't want to be confronted in a match with a situation he couldn't handle. The only way to preclude that was to spend more time on the mat than anyone in the world, with anyone who would wrestle with him. He took on teammates in practice one after another without breaking to rest. When one became tired, the next stepped in. Weight didn't matter.

The workout routine varied so Gable wouldn't "bore" himself. He ran as many as 10 miles a day encased in a plastic suit to increase sweating, often paced by a friend in a car with the radio playing country music. On the way back, the heater went on maximum for instant sauna.

He'd pick a card from a deck and match the number on it with push-ups. Joker was highest; that "cost" Gable 16 push-ups. He tried to see how many times he could go through the entire deck without stopping.

High school and college students became used to seeing

Gable run from class to class with five- or 10-pound weights strapped to his wrists and ankles and wearing a 10-pound weighted vest.

Any workout Gable began was always carried several steps beyond his endurance. He'd run in the morning, get wobbly at five miles, then push for several more before he'd allow himself to quit. When he lifted weights, he'd go two or three additional sets after the pain began.

"When I lifted weights, I didn't lift just to maintain my muscle tone," he told me. "I lifted to increase what I already had, to push to a new limit. Every time I worked, I was getting a little better. I kept moving that limit back and back. Every time I walked out of the gym, I was a little bit better than when I walked in.

"By the end of practice, I wanted to be physically tired, to know that I'd really been through a workout," he said. "If I wasn't tired, I must have cheated somehow, so I stayed a little longer." Any time Gable got up in the morning and wasn't tired, he considered the previous day's workout a waste.

"When I'd get tired and want to stop, I'd wonder what my next opponent was doing. I'd wonder if he was still working out. I tried to visualize him. When I could *see* him still working, I'd start pushing myself. When I could *see* him in the shower, I'd push myself harder."

When his teammates rested, Gable worked. When they watched TV, he worked. When they had parties, he worked. When they dated, he worked.

"Soon the guys on my team knew what I was doing. More important, my opponents heard what I was doing," Dan said. "And when my opponents got on the mat with me, I had that edge. They started scared.

"You've got to have a tough *mind*. If you know you haven't cheated physically in your preparation, that makes you mentally tough." What made *him* mentally tough was knowing—when he faced anybody—that the other guy would give out before he would.

(Even the police couldn't stop Gable from working out. Standing on the sidewalk in front of his college apartment one evening talking with a friend and holding a paper cup with a bit of beer in it, Gable was stopped and questioned by a policeman. He argued and was taken to the station and jailed. When his friends got there to get him out, they found Gable calmly chinning himself on a pipe that ran through the cell.)

Gable set goals—often creating them when none existed—and then sweated to reach them. During his junior year in college, he considered the national competition in his weight inadequate for him, so he went up one weight to meet an undefeated national champion from the University of Oklahoma. His sole reason: the challenge of another superb wrestler. Dan won decisively.

Dan talks in "odd" phrases. Odd in that they are sometimes clichés. Only, when Dan says them, the moss falls off because they come from the lips of a man who has demonstrated since boyhood that he means every one of them. They're phrases like "desire to win," "never quit," "just battle your heart out," "get out there and go," "why train at all if you're not going to do your best?"

After Gable graduated from Iowa State in 1971, he increased his workouts to 6 hours a day, aiming toward the Olympics. He had been undefeated in 181 consecutive matches through seven years of high school and collegiate wrestling. He lost only one match, his last intercollegiate competition, by two points to Larry Owings, a man he had beaten before and defeated since.

Gable's basement is a miniature gym with wrestling mat, weights of myriad types and a hot box. During the months before the 1972 Olympics, dozens of wrestlers from throughout the country—including arch-rival Oklahomans—came to spend varying times working out with Dan, bleeding him of his knowledge, absorbing his techniques. They came from rural towns in New England, from metropolitan areas like New York and Chicago, from the South and California. Everyone wanted to match his best against Dan and to learn from the man who seemed to have perfected the art of wrestling. The Gables bought their beef by the half-cow and milk in five-gallon tanks.

I know a number of tightly knit families, genuinely devoted and caring about each other. But Dan's family is entitled to one-half of the trophies Dan has ever won.

When Dan was a boy he was well on the way to becoming a Class A monster. By the time he was four, his parents began to think he was incorrigible. His language was blue and his misdeeds violent. One day shortly before his fifth birthday, he went on a shopping trip with his mother. While she was browsing through a rack of skirts, Dan spotted a well-padded woman shopper bending over a low-cased display. Dan snuck up on her and gleefully bit her on her rump. (Dan's rump became sore that night.)

His father decided Dan needed an outlet for his energy. Mack Gable thought of athletics for Dan and turned his son on to a way of life that channeled his energy into the creation of a one of a kind champion.

Baseball and football were too slow for Dan. He tried swimming—and became a winner. In his third year of competition—he was 10—Dan was undefeated in the backstroke. Then he won the district qualifying tournament and the state championship. The title sent Dan to represent Iowa in a regional YMCA meet in Iowa City.

Unexpectedly, Dan lost—to a teammate he had beaten frequently. But even at that age, Dan knew himself. He realized "that other guy had found his sport. I hadn't found mine." Dan needed a more personal kind of sport, one that offered greater contact. He would try wrestling.

By the time he was in junior high school, the wrestling "craze" had hit northeast Iowa. Mack Gable encouraged his son's interest in wrestling. (He had wrestled in high school in the 105-pound class and had met Dan's mother, Katie, during a wrestling match; her brother, a teammate, introduced them.) Mack was Dan's most ardent booster. He attended every match, even wrestled with Dan for practice until Dan began to beat him consistently.

When Dan broke a finger wrestling in junior high school, his doctor put it in a cast and told him not to work out. Dan had to return to the doctor three times for new casts because he kept breaking them in workouts.

Just as Mack was always there when Dan needed him, Gable's mother, Katie, was the heart and soul of this competitive family. She would never let Dan "cop out." She set high standards. When Dan was 12 and became apprehensive one day about a match with a tough opponent whose reputation had preceded him, it was Katie who challenged Dan.

"What a lily," she mused, just clearly enough for Dan to overhear in the next room. "Not even face to face with his opponent and he's already a loser."

Another time, when Dan seemed discouraged and fear took over, Katie was overheard saying to no one in particular (the only other person in the room was Dan), "I'm going to trade in his wrestling shoes for a pair of ballet slippers and a leotard. He's not a wrestler. We'll see if he can learn to dance."

His mother never had to make comments like those again.

Dan weighed 127 pounds as a ninth-grader. He judged his

best chance as a wrestler that fall to be at 95 pounds although he could probably wrestle well at the heavier weight. It was an "impossible" goal.

Thanksgiving wasn't a feast day at the Gable home that year. The famine was observed by the whole family. Katie proclaimed no meal could be cooked during Dan's crash-diet ordeal. During this period of starvation, Mack would sneak downtown whenever his hunger pains became unendurable and stuff himself at the nearest diner. Katie caught Diane wolfing down a piece of pie behind a closed closet door. Dan never relaxed his starvation program. He began to look like a prisoner-of-war victim. But he made the weight. In dropping from 127 to 95 pounds, Dan sacrificed over 20 percent of his gross body weight. He would never attempt that again, however. Trainers and physicians agree that an athlete in training should drop no more than eight percent of his gross body weight.

I wondered if Gable's intensity caused him to be ridiculed by classmates. "Oh no, we admired him immensely," Marty Dickey, a former teammate and also a high school state wrestling champion, told me. "He was an example to all of us. Anyone who wants to can get up at 5:30 or 6:00 in the morning and run three or four miles before class. But how many do it?

"He's proof that if you work hard enough, practice long enough, you can reach the top. If someone, say a wrestler, works on a move 1,000 times, he's going to be able to do it better than someone who practiced it 100 times. Then someone like Dan who practiced it 100,000 times comes along; that's why he handled the Russians so easily."

I asked Gable what drove him to work out so hard. He said he wanted to be the Olympic champion and the only way he could do that was work. "You can't ever work too much because there's no such thing as being in too good condition. You can't ever lift too many weights because you can't ever get too strong. You can't ever wrestle too much because you can *always* do better."

You can always do better. Australian John Landy, the world's second man to break the four-minute mile, did it only after deciding that overtraining was a fiction and that the more the body endures, the more it will endure.

What did Gable's friends and classmates think of his single-minded dedication?

"I didn't care what they thought. I had only one thing in mind."

But every now and then, Gable would tell me: "People thought I was crazy" or "Everyone thought there was something wrong with me." At the world competition in Sofia, a six-time world champion from Iran walked up to an American wrestler after watching Gable work out for a day or two and asked, "Is there something wrong with his mentality?"

Gable not only won in his class in the Olympics, he fired up the American free-style team to win six medals, the best our country has ever done.

I covered that event for ABC television and after becoming close to the U.S. team, I frankly felt that without Gable there would have been no medals at all. He had that much influence on his teammates.

This influence was most obvious in the case of the Peterson brothers. A gold medal was taken in the 198-pound class by Ben Peterson and a silver medal in the 180.4 pound class by Ben's brother, John.

Neither had had any major accomplishment in wrestling before he met Gable. Ben enrolled as a freshman at Iowa State when Gable was a junior there. John, older than Gable, became Dan's roommate for the year before the Olympic trials.

Neither of the Petersons was expected to win a place on the Olympic team. Three months before the trials for the Olympics, Ben Peterson was beaten, 10–0, by a former national champion. John Peterson was defeated, 15–0, by a member of the 1968 Olympic team. But at the trials, Ben and John ran through everyone. Both came out of the middle ranks of American wrestling to make the squad, then astonished everyone again by winning medals.

Both young men had ability—Gable believes they had more natural strength than he—but neither had ever worked enough to develop his talent. Face to face with Gable, they were able to see what had to be done. Both adopted Gable's training methods, probably exceeded his pace for a time because they had so many years to make up for. John improved so quickly, Gable says, "that it was unbelievable; all that talent waiting to be used."

"Ben had a lot to learn when he came to Iowa State," he continued. "He wasn't very good. But he had the desire. He'd get beat, get right up and go back at his opponent. Pretty soon he wasn't getting beat as much. Then he was winning all the time.

"He realized what it took—and that desire got him the Olympic medal."

Gable ripped a cartilage in his left knee when he was working out in college with someone 70 pounds heavier than he, Two years later, the knee ripped again. (That workout, incidentally, was at 11:00 P.M.) The Olympic trials were two months away. Physicians urged an operation, but none would give a guarantee of full recovery for the trials.

Gable taped his knee and kept working. Characteristically, he says he gained because he was forced to learn to wrestle favoring the bad knee. "I never would have learned those new methods if my knee hadn't been hurt."

After the Olympics, Gable was working out on the mat

when the knee locked. He couldn't straighten it. The operation was the next morning. A month later, the other knee, which had been bothering him sporadically, worsened and an operation to repair it followed. He had wrestled with both bad knees through the world tournament and the Olympics.

When I talk with other wrestlers who have been exposed to Dan, I realize I'm repeatedly hearing Gable's philosophy. They're not parroting. He's piling up converts by the dozens.

Gable is a magnet for American wrestlers at the University of Iowa, where he is now an assistant coach. Jay Robinson, a member of the 1972 Olympic team and a graduate of the University of Oklahoma, one of the greatest wrestling schools in the nation, came to Iowa as an unpaid graduate assistant because Gable was there.

"Five men who plan to try for the 1976 Olympics are here as graduate assistants," Robinson told me. "Every one of us has come here because of Gable. Because we can work with him directly and we know he'll help us any way he can.

"I didn't know anything about the University of Iowa before. It wasn't a wrestling power. Oklahoma State, the University of Oklahoma, Iowa State, and a few other colleges were *the* schools for wrestling.

"I could have gone back to the University of Oklahoma. Its wrestling team had won the national NCAA title most of the 45 years the NCAAs have existed. But the University of Iowa won in 1975 and 1976 and was ranked first in the nation. A lot of that credit has to go to Gable.

"I'm two years older than Gable, but he's an inspiration to me. I lived across the street from him here for a while and it took my *seeing* his daily routine to really understand how much he does. He doesn't wrestle competitively now. But he still works at it as if he had a meet tomorrow."

Gable and a group of friends were watching a Russian basketball team play a U.S. team on television one evening.

After it was over, everyone except Gable piled into a car to get a beer. Gable put his sweat suit on—it was 1:00 A.M.—and ran three miles.

Gable tells team members and the graduate assistants he'll work with them any time they want: 6:00 A.M., noon, 2:00 A.M. Dan often is at school at midnight jumping rope and lifting weights *in* the hotbox.

"Watching Gable makes us understand *we* can do more," said Robinson. "We all work hard; you don't qualify for the Olympics unless you do. But Gable makes us realize we're capable of giving more. He's teaching us by example that no one ever fully taps his reservoir of potential."

Many athletes think they're dedicating themselves to their sport, but when they get around Gable and they see how much more *he* is doing, they dig deeper within themselves. They may think they can run only two miles, see Gable run three or four and say, "Well, maybe I can, too."

"Some of the kids here used to go just to the standard one a day practice," Robinson said. "But now a lot work out on the mat in the morning. They'll run, they'll play paddle ball, come back for mat practice in the afternoon, run or play some more paddle ball in the evening. All because of Gable.

"Dan also teaches them to think: not I *hope* I can make the Olympic team, but I *will* make the Olympic team. Nothing can stop me."

I recently had dinner with an old friend. His wife and two sons listened to us reminisce about some of the all-time sports greats. As I mentioned Dan Gable, I thought one of the boys would explode right out of his chair.

"Do you know Dan Gable?" Steve demanded. "God, was he my hero when I was on the freshman wrestling team. I was a little kid, too short for basketball, too skinny for football, too knock-kneed and pigeon-toed for track. I tried out for wrestling.

"I was terrible when I started. But I tried. If Dan Gable said I could do it by the example of the way *he* worked— and he 'said' it to every kid on every wrestling team across the country—I had to try. I made the freshman team. I went to a wrestling clinic that summer and then I made varsity.

"Maybe if I had stuck to it like Gable, I might have been something. I had three body-building, mind-disciplining years on the wrestling team and I learned a hell of a lot about competition."

Steve is now in graduate school, majoring in education. He told me of a recent interview he had had for a teaching job. He thinks he might have an edge for the job in today's competitive teaching market because he can also coach wrestling. The school, a small private one, is thinking of starting a wrestling program for its sixty boys.

I'll put it to *you:* How can a man who is a hero to thousands of "average" kids across the country not be an outstanding example of the best that sports has to offer?

Gable agrees he is a fanatic, that wrestling has been an obsession with him—and then he grins. Noncompetitor now or not, he clearly has no intention of changing.

When Gable returned from the Olympics, he told a group of high school students, "I was no different when I was your age than you are right this minute. I won because I was willing to do the work necessary to win. Find your goal in life and then go get it."

Sir Edmund Hillary, the first man to climb Mount Everest, put it another way: "You don't have to be a fantastic sort of hero to do certain things. You can be just an ordinary chap, sufficiently motivated, to reach challenging goals. (And) the intense effort, the giving everything you've got . . . is a very pleasant bonus."

Joe Greene, unanimous All-Pro defensive tackle of the

Pittsburgh Steelers for the last three seasons, was subtly self-critical when he told a writer he is waiting for a special game: "A game where I don't miss a tackle, where I and everyone around me do everything to the absolute letter of perfection. I *do* have that game in my repertoire and until that time I will not be fulfilled."

Dan Gable would understand Joe in an instant.

Willis
Reed

They called him captain. He was their big man, not big by the skewed standards of the sport they played, but because he was their indispensable one. In basketball vernacular, the center position is called the pivot. For far more than merely filling that spot, he *was* the pivot of the New York Knicks. He was the man around whom a once-terrible team had finally jelled and was now fighting for a title.

They called him captain—and they meant it. Bradley, the Rhodes Scholar by way of Princeton University; Barnett, the oldest member of the team, cynic, funmaker; Frazier, soon to be called one of the best guards in the National Basketball Association. DeBusschere, the final part of a puzzle that, assembled, had brought New York to the brink of a championship.

For much of its history, New York had been a joke in the league. But now, in the fifth game of the 1969–70 playoff finals, it was a joke no longer. Hungry for their first championship, tied with Los Angeles at two games each in a best of seven series, the Knicks had just returned from California to their home court in Madison Square Garden. And their chances depended greatly on their captain, Willis Reed, not only for his offensive strength but also to neutralize 7'1" Wilt

Chamberlain, the top scorer and best rebounder ever to play professional basketball.

And then Reed fell. Driving for a basket with only eight minutes played, with no one near, he suddenly collapsed and lay still. In 28 years of playing and covering sports, I've seen countless injuries. But I will never forget Reed's face that night, grotesquely twisted in pain. Suddenly, the quest of the Knicks and of Willis Reed had pulled up short.

In the northern Louisiana farm country where he was born, he could tell early that basketball was his sport. It took him a little longer to realize it would also be his economic passport. He fashioned two hoops for his backyard and, year round, often wearing a heavy coat and sweaters in the cold months, spent hours throwing a basketball through them.

He grew big quickly, courtesy of his father's side of the family. He was 6'2" when school let out for the summer after eighth grade, 6'5" when classes resumed that September.

In the segregated high school in Bernice, with only 50 boys in the entire building, it wasn't hard for the coach to find, and draft, the growing ninth-grader for the basketball team. But all Coach Lendon Stone got at the moment was size. Sprouting so fast that he grew into and out of his father's clothes before he could try them on, Willis Reed had difficulty walking down the road. His own feet frequently tripped him.

Perhaps because Stone saw some flicker of raw talent in this huge, awkward youngster or maybe because no basketball coach in a tiny school casts off someone taller than most men, Stone decided to work with Reed. He started at the pre-primer level. He gave Reed a jump rope and ordered him to use it 20 minutes a day to improve his coordination. He taught Reed how to hold a ball, dribble, pass. Reed had a nice, soft touch with a shot. But that was the only natural gift he had.

"I was the tallest kid in school and probably the worst

player," he was to say. "I was clumsy, didn't know how to move, and knew practically nothing about the fundamentals of the game. Coach Stone took a 13-year-old nothing who was frightened every time he had to go out on a court and made him into some kind of athlete. Without him, I would never have gone anywhere."

A man any thoughtful parent would like to have instruct his children, Stone worked on Reed's head as well as on his athletic skills. Caught jumping up and jamming the ball into the basket one day—a feat requiring no talent, just sufficient height—Reed heard: "Dad-blame-it, you can't hold a basketball, you can't catch a basketball, you can't even run up and down the court and here you are showing off, dunking the ball." (Reed was later to tell me, "Some kids would have taken that as an insult. I sure didn't. I was nowhere close to being a basketball player. He wanted me to realize that I had a lot of work to do. And he *made* me work harder to prove I was more than a show-off, that I could learn the finer points of the game."')

Reed threw a childish tantrum one afternoon when a referee made a call that displeased him. Before the official could heave Reed out of the game and call a technical foul, Stone was off the bench. "Get dressed," he said to Reed. "Until you can act like a man, you won't play for this team."

There was of course little money at home and Reed had to look for jobs as soon as he was old enough. As he edged into adolescence, he often worked alongside family men, did the same work, and was paid the same poor wage. Both of his parents worked hard—his father as a truckdriver, his mother as a field hand and, later, a domestic in town. Reed sometimes worked the cotton rows with his mother.

"You can't know what that's like unless you've done it," Reed told me. "Blistering heat. Dust swirling. Ants in the drinking water. The 'hands' crawling down the cotton rows on their knees grabbing the bolls and throwing them into huge sacks they dragged behind them."

It was about then that he understood that basketball was his only route out of a future that would otherwise force him to do "what all the black men in Bernice did for a living." "After my second year in high school, I knew I could play well enough to get a scholarship to college, and that that was the only way I was going to get there. Basketball stopped being a game to me then."

For Reed, as for me, sports were an avenue to a vastly different life than either of us would have led had we not been fortunate enough to have been given physical skills we could develop. Basketball took Reed out of the rural, black South— a ghetto by any definition—and made him a superstar. Football did much the same for me. The oil fields of the Southwest and West were replaced by Yankee Stadium.

So much in common in spite of our very different backgrounds. Reed talks of those "willing to pay the price" and those with far more natural talent than he, who were not. They are still in Louisiana, endlessly talking of what might have been.

"There were boys ahead of me in school who were fine athletes, who could have played college or pro ball, but they just didn't *do* anything; they just stayed around home. I said I wasn't going to let that happen to me. If I failed at something, it would be because I didn't have the ability, not because I didn't give 100 percent of what I had. Not because I wasn't willing to pay the price."

Reed paid the price: hours of lonely practice in the school gym long after others had gone home, in his yard as a growing, gangly boy, where he fought to gain mastery of his body and to learn to do things with a ball that perhaps only a dozen big men in his time would learn.

He often despaired. He watched older athletes in high school and college—tall men, for they were the only ones he compared himself to—do things on the court that he could not. Men in his hometown, hearing praise for the only child of Willis and Inell Reed, who was scoring 30, 40, and 50 points a game, scoffed and said he was able to do what he did only because he happened to be tall and there was no skill involved. I know the "same" men. They exist everywhere. The quick to criticize, quick to bring down. One man, almost as close to me as a member of my family, told me I would never succeed either as a runner or pass receiver in college and professional football. And I almost listened to him.

Reed could do nothing about that kind of talk and his own frustrations except work harder. Coach Stone and assistant coach Duke Fields helped sustain him. Fields repeatedly would tell Reed, "Reach for the sky and if you miss, you've got to get a star"; "There'll always be times in the race when you'll fall. If you get up, brush yourself off and start running again. You can catch up and still win."

Corny? Not to an adolescent worrying if and where he'll fit into a world that is oblivious to him. A young man growing up needs a vision as he tries to sort out his future and Stone and Fields in different ways supplied them for Reed. My high school football coach in Bakersfield, California, Homer Beatty, did the same thing for me. He drew my eyes from the oil rigs I saw as my certain future after high school and sketched goals for me that had not at all seemed possible before.

Reed speaks of giving 100 percent. "Any guy I worked for would tell you one thing: *I worked*. No one had to watch me. Even as a kid. When I weeded flower beds for the white ladies, I sweated until I got every bit of grass out and made it as pretty as I could. Whatever I agreed to do, I did. I didn't care what the amount of money was or whether I had made a good deal or a bad deal; if I had an obligation, I completed it."

The word spreads when a high school sophomore who is 6'6" and still growing is scoring bunches of baskets. One spring afternoon near the end of his second year in high school, as Reed and a friend waited in a nearby town to take a bus home, a man walked up to Reed and asked his name. He introduced himself as Fred Hobdy, basketball coach at nearby Grambling College. On the spot, Hobdy told Reed he had a scholarship to Grambling when he finished high school. The offer wasn't as casual as it seemed. Hobdy had been following Reed's progress. He had even made a minor investment in his team's future. Through Lendon Stone, he had been supplying Grambling sneakers for Reed, whose feet were too large for boys' basketball shoes.

Reed was anxious to get to college because he wanted to find out how good a basketball player he was. His high school team had won a state title in Reed's senior year and he was the star. "But I had no way of knowing if I really could play. We were matched only against other small, black high schools. I never competed against white players. I had no way of knowing how good a 17-year-old in California or New York or St. Louis or anywhere else in the country was."

Although colleges from Texas to Illinois offered him scholarships, he selected Grambling. "I really chose Coach Hobdy, a man I had seen take players my size and teach them to do things I couldn't do." Success causes greater hungers. Television had brought the pros to Louisiana and Reed selected an idol, a left-handed center like himself who could not tolerate defeat, Bill Russell of the Boston Celtics. Could he, Reed wondered, someday play pro ball?

Colleges recruited them as now—avariciously. Coaches coaxed, wheedled, lied, bribed. Grambling didn't. "Grambling was different from most of the schools that wanted me," Reed said. "Some promised that I could walk right in and be a starter. The only thing Coach Hobdy promised was that I would get a chance to play."

There were no injunctions at Grambling against Reed jumping up and dunking the ball. He was ordered to do it about a dozen times each day. One afternoon, Reed pushed a hook shot toward the basket, dodged around his defender, grabbed the rebound with one hand and went high to shove the ball through the net. He turned to run up court when Hobdy, watching in the stands, called him over and told him he would be an All-American before he graduated.

Four years at Grambling transformed Reed into one of the nation's best college athletes. The basketball team won 108 games, lost only 17 during his four years. He scored 2,315 points during regular-season play and averaged better than 22 points a game in national small-college tournaments. He was named to virtually every Little All-American team his junior and senior years.

As he would with New York, Reed played with deep, hurting pain at Grambling. In his biography, *Willis Reed,* writer Larry Fox recalled one game when Reed, playing "virtually one-handed" because of a severe shoulder injury sustained the night before, scored 30 points. Reed missed only three games in his entire college career.

No longer the awkward, uncertain athlete, he was now a proud, quietly confident man. He waited calmly for the professional basketball draft, certain he would be picked in the first round by one of the nine clubs that then comprised the NBA. The Knicks, who had first choice by virtue of having had the worst record in the league the year before, agonized over the big man they badly needed. They narrowed the choice to three: Jim "Bad News" Barnes of Texas Western, Luke Jackson of Pan-American, and Reed.

The Knicks believed Reed had "the greatest future" of the three, but that it would take him longer to develop. They chose Barnes because they thought he would be able to play pro ball sooner. Jackson was taken fourth. When it was New York's turn again at the start of the second round, Reed was still available and the Knicks grabbed him.

"Perhaps it was the disappointment of not being selected in

the first round that prompted Reed . . . to work hard to make it big in the NBA," said sportswriter Phil Pepe. "If that was the case, getting picked in the second round was a stroke of good luck—not only for the Knicks but for Reed as well. . . . Minor setbacks bring out the best in him. For most of his life, he has combated each crisis with the same remedy—hard work and determination."

Once again, Reed had skeptics and something to prove. He did, quickly. By the end of training camp, he was the first-string center, displacing Barnes. At midseason he was picked for the All-Star game, the first of seven consecutive years he would be chosen. By the end of the year, he was the league's Rookie of the Year and the Knicks' high scorer.

"Desire can 'rewrite' all your scouting reports," Gil Brandt, director of player personnel for the Dallas Cowboys, once said. "You can spend millions of dollars evaluating players, but if there were only some way you could find out how much desire a boy has to excel, it would make the job easy. This is the one thing left to chance. Some boys rise; others don't."

"I knew I was coming into the league an underrated player," Reed said. "But I believed I could play in the NBA. I said that when I signed my contract. I was told that a lot of All-Americans had said the same thing and hadn't been able to produce. I was determined to produce."

The Knicks had never had a Rookie of the Year. They also had not had a winning season for five years and had missed the championship playoffs eight of the prior nine seasons. Reed was to change all that.

Reed, the child, weeding gardens in Bernice, worked hard. Reed, the grown man, worked as hard in the NBA. He became, I believe, one of the most "honest" players in the league. Honest in sports means giving all you can all the time. Reed went on the floor every game prepared to play not 12 or 24 minutes but a full 48, if necessary. Not all basketball players do that over an 82-game schedule. It's difficult to get yourself "up" for each game, especially for big men like Reed who play a bruising game.

He quickly showed he wasn't adverse to using his strength and 245 pounds to best advantage, heritage perhaps from his all-state football days in high school when he realized "contact wouldn't hurt." Reed intimidated his opponents. "He plays his man very close," wrote Arnold Hano, "muscling him, pushing, hooking an arm inside his foe's arms, blocking his man off the boards. He probably plays as close a defense as any big man in the league." He was to have his nose broken five times in basketball and develop scar tissue around both eyes.

Reed didn't hesitate to "take care of business" if it came to a fight. There was one memorable night in New York's old Madison Square Garden when Reed took on the entire Laker team. Punched by a Laker, Reed went after him and then anyone in the club. He broke one man's jaw and knocked out two others. Players ran just to get out of his way. "Few NBA players," noted one sportswriter, "ever challenged him again."

Even though Reed had been elected Rookie of the Year and led the Knicks in scoring, New York's management was still experimenting, still trying to put together a winning team. They wanted a bigger man at center and Reed, whose listed height was 6'10", was just a shade over 6'8", small by the standards then. New York traded three players, including Barnes, to Baltimore for 6'11" Walt Bellamy.

Reed had to leave the position he had worked so hard to learn and move to forward. It was a totally new job. He wasn't happy, but in his customary way worked hard to adjust. He was already setting an example that several seasons later would characterize a "new" Knick ball club, a team that was extraordinarily unselfish and worked as a unit offensively and defensively with an effectiveness—and a grace—never before seen in the NBA.

The move to forward was a difficult adjustment. Yet Reed

did it so well that he was chosen again for the All-Star game, the first player in the league to be selected at two positions. The league was expanding and that complicated the transition. With only nine teams, it wasn't uncommon to have forwards as big as Reed. As more teams were added, however, talent thinned out and smaller men began to play forward. Reed often found himself guarding men two or three inches shorter and eventually he began to look slow in contrast with those smaller, more agile players.

The Bellamy trade didn't work. The Knicks improved little. In 1968, Bellamy's fourth season with New York, he went to Detroit in an early-season trade that brought Dave DeBusschere to New York.

Reed relinquished forward to DeBusschere and moved back to center. The change was a revelation. The man who had looked slow and plodding at forward "suddenly" became cat-quick and one of the most mobile centers in the league. He was a forerunner of the "small" center. He proved a team could win with a center his size.

Reed was happy again. "The burden is on me now. But I like it that way. I like it when I'm responsible for the team effort."

"If there's a key to Willis Reed," wrote Fox, "perhaps this is it: he takes responsibility. And if this makes his stomach churn and his temper shorten, it also makes him more of a man."

An unusual man. His unselfishness and sense of personal responsibility made him a natural leader. He would take the blame for some losses as if there were no other players on the team. He had caused his high school to lose one state championship, he said, because he had taken a play from a basketball magazine and used it incorrectly. He didn't add that he alone brought the team to the state final. He would later believe that a shoulder injury he sustained during the 1970–71 season "hurt the Knicks and made the difference between its winning the league title and losing it."

He roomed with rookies—white or black, uncommon in sports' special ways of segregation—after he had been named the Knicks' captain in his fourth season because he thought he could help them. He had knocked on the coach's door at the start of his rookie year to ask for a league rule book. Asked why, Reed said, "How can I play if I don't know the rules?" Simple question; simple answer; yet Reed is probably the only rookie known to have done this.

He wanted others to share his limelight. In high school his senior year, he had asked that someone else be captain of the football team. He had been captain his junior year. "I wanted some other guys to feel they're important to the team, too," he told me.

When football plays were designed to use Reed, an end, as a decoy, Reed thought that made a lot of sense. He knew he wouldn't play football after high school, but the other end might and could use the experience and the publicity. (Reed had been "drafted" for football in high school, too, and soon became the team's star. "I caught a three-yard pass and simply fell forward and we had a first down," he wisecracked to me as we compared memories of high school ball.)

The DeBusschere trade made Reed and the Knicks and finally gave New York the combination it needed to win. Bill Bradley and Walt Frazier had already been obtained in the college draft and Dick Barnett through a trade. The Knicks finished the 1968–69 season by winning 36 of their last 47 games.

They then blitzed the Baltimore Bullets, who had finished first in the Eastern Division, in four straight games in the first round of the playoffs.

Bill Russell, playing his last season, and the Celtics were

too much and eliminated New York in the second round of the playoffs. But the Knicks knew they were now a winner. So did basketball fans as they began to jam the Garden to capacity.

The next season belonged to the Knicks from the start.

"Right now, after less than two weeks of training camp, our offense is incredibly smooth," DeBusschere wrote in his diary of the 1969–70 season, *The Open Man.* "We know each other so well. Bradley senses where Frazier is without even looking for him. Frazier senses where Willis is. It's a beautiful thing to watch. Red (Coach Red Holzman) keeps yelling at us, 'Look for the open man,' and most of the time we do. . . . We keep moving until one of us is open and then somebody hits him and he gets a clear shot.

". . . The big thing is we're playing unselfish basketball. We're always thinking about the other guy. It's funny; for most of us, it goes completely against the way we grew up playing basketball. Every single one of us . . . was *the* star of his high school team . . . and each of us was expected to do everything, from shooting to playmaking to rebounding. We were encouraged to freelance because at least 99 percent of the time we were better than the men guarding us. We were encouraged to be individuals.

"And *now* we're encouraged to be a team, to work together, to take as much pride in setting a good pick [a legal, stationary block that allows someone else to get free] as in scoring a basket. It's against our basketball nature, but we're doing it more and more every day. The game is still 75 percent freelance, but it's that other 25 percent, our teamwork . . . that just might separate us from the rest of the league."

DeBusschere described a game the Knicks played early in the season. It was the rookie year for Lew Alcindor, the 7'2" Milwaukee center who would change his name to Kareem Abdul-Jabbar. New York had won its first game of the year against Milwaukee by four points.

After reporters left the room, Reed brought the team together. ". . . We're getting ready to leave on our first real road trip. You know what happened last year. On our first . . . trip, we lost five out of six games and it turned our whole season around. . . . I know I didn't do much tonight [he got into foul trouble early], but I'm gonna go out on the road trip and I'm gonna play ball every minute and I want *everybody* playing ball every minute."

The first stop was Milwaukee for the second of back-to-back games. The Bucks were in second place in the division and New York in first.

". . . The game started and Willis took over," DeBusschere wrote. "Willy's amazing. I don't think he ever plays two bad games in a row, and the poorer he plays one night, the better he plays the next. He's not one of the bigger centers but he's one of the strongest and he blends his strength with the best outside touch of all the centers—a . . . jump shot that he perfected during the years he played forward for the Knicks and Bellamy played center.

"Willy gave Alcindor lessons tonight at both ends of the court. Once, for instance, he faked a jump shot and as Lew went up to block it, Willy twisted around him and drove in for a layup. A minute later, Willy faked the drive, edging Lew back, then jumped, his legs tucked under him, uncoiled and sank a long jumper.

"On defense, Willis kept shoving his chest against Lew's back, forcing him away from the basket, forcing him to take his hook shots and jump shots a little farther away from the basket than he likes.

". . . Willy and I had one play working beautifully. It's a play where everybody clears out one side of the court and leaves it open for me to go one-on-one on my man. Except I don't really go one-on-one. I dribble toward the baseline, Willis slides by me, and I sort of hand him the ball and (block) his man. Then he jumps and shoots. I think we tried that play four times . . . and it worked four times." New York won easily.

Little, it seemed, could go wrong. The Knicks won 22 of their first 23 games and set an NBA record of 18 consecutive victories. They defeated Atlanta to tie the old record of 17. The Knicks outplayed Atlanta in the third quarter, 32–12. It was one of the best quarters of pro basketball ever played. "I was embarrassed by it," said Atlanta coach Richie Guerin. "I've never seen anything like it before and I don't think I ever will again."

New York won its 18th straight against Cincinnati. With 16 seconds left to play, New York was losing by five points. Reed hit two free throws to cut the lead to three. Bob Cousy, one of pro basketball's spectacular "small" men at 6′1″ and at 41 the Cincinnati player-coach, had put himself in to play. On an inbound pass, Cousy threw the ball to forward Tom Van Arsdale, but DeBusschere intercepted and drove for two points. Ten seconds remained. The Knicks trailed by one.

Cincinnati again put the ball in play, intending to hold it until time ran out. Reed and Frazier double-teamed Van Arsdale. Reed slapped the ball loose, Frazier grabbed it, raced downcourt for the layup, missed, took the rebound, missed again, then was fouled at the game-ending buzzer. He made both shots to put New York up, 106–105.

From third place in their division the two prior years, only two seasons removed from last place, the Knicks were clearly headed for the division title, their first in 16 years. It was to be Reed's greatest season. Although he began to feel the effects of tendonitis in his left knee, the result of bouncing 245 pounds on hardwood floors, he didn't let it affect his play. He led New York in scoring and in rebounding.

In the first round of the playoffs, he put on one of the best demonstrations of basketball I've ever seen. That entire series, matching New York with the Baltimore Bullets, was extra-ordinary. New York won the first two games. Baltimore fought back to capture the next two. The fifth game clearly would give the winner an extraordinary emotional lift. And Willis Reed decided it. Reed scored 36 points and took 36 rebounds —a Knick record—in the fifth game to lead New York to a 3–2 edge in games. Just before the game ended, Holzman took Reed, Frazier, and DeBusschere out at the same time. The Garden crowd stood for a two-minute ovation, most of it clearly directed at Reed. Baltimore won the sixth game and the Knicks, led by Reed, the deciding seventh. He hit on better than 50 percent of his shots from 20 feet out, unusual for a center.

The Knicks won four games of five from Milwaukee to qualify for the final round against the Los Angeles Lakers with Wilt Chamberlain and Jerry West. Chamberlain, too, had knee trouble. He had undergone surgery in November and re-turned for the playoffs.

The Lakers wanted the title badly. They were a proud, and a superb team. But they had yet to win a league title. They had reached the playoff finals six times in the prior eight years, losing on each occasion. Three of those times they got to the seventh game and lost by less than three points.

Reed led both teams in scoring in the first game with 37 points. The Knicks won. Los Angeles took the second, New York, the third in overtime, and the Lakers the fourth, again in overtime. The series returned to New York for the fifth game. Los Angeles would be the site of the sixth game and New York the seventh if the series went that far.

Then it happened. Eight minutes into the first quarter of the fifth game, Reed raced around Chamberlain, headed for the basket—and dropped as if he had been hit with an ax handle. His first thought as he lay on the floor in front of 19,500 stilled fans and a nationwide television audience including his par-

ents was *We've come so far and it's over*. At midcourt, De-
Busschere stared and whispered, "Oh, my God. Oh, no." ("I
could see our championship lying on the floor," he was to
write. "I could see our chances disappearing in pain. I could
see the whole year crumbling with Willis' . . . leg.")

Reed tried to stand and pain ripped through his thigh. He
wanted to play, but had to leave the floor. It was a badly
strained muscle in his right thigh. His right leg had been
pushed too far in favoring his left knee. In the locker room,
Reed was given shots of cortisone and then painkiller, but
neither had much effect. He couldn't play the second half. Los
Angeles led at the half, 53–40. Three different players had
tried to contain Chamberlain, but Wilt made seven of the
Lakers' first 10 points after Reed left the game.

The Lakers were sure to increase their 13-point advantage
in the second half with relative ease. During the halftime
break, Bradley suggested an old offensive pattern that would,
hopefully, keep one Knick free and make maximum use of the
ability of each member of the team to score from 20–25 feet
out. Holzman told his players "to go out and create a little
havoc." Forward Cazzie Russell beseeched the Knicks to win
"for the captain after all the times he's bailed us out."

And, somehow, in an extraordinary team effort, New York
did it. They did create havoc as Reed, in the dressing room,
listened to a play-by-play account relayed over the telephone
by public-address announcer, John Condon. With no one
taller than 6'7" on the floor, the Knicks outrebounded Los
Angeles in the second half, 22 to 18, and outscored them 67–
47. The Lakers found themselves short in every department.
They were able to get off only 26 shots in the second half; the
Knicks, 57. The Lakers lost the ball to New York's aggressive
defense 10 times in the final quarter; the Knicks lost none.
Chamberlain scored only four points.

New York now had a 3–2 game lead and a one-game cushion. There were two days before the sixth game in Los Angeles, four before the seventh back in New York. The question became: Could Reed, the league's Most Valuable Player and the Knicks' leading scorer, recover for either of those games? If he couldn't, how would New York do without him? There were no illusions that the Knicks could duplicate the fifth game where they won without him.

Reed didn't even put on his uniform for the sixth game. He visited a doctor before the game and tried an experimental jump to touch the ceiling. He got off on his good leg. He landed on his right—and almost passed out from the pain. Barely able to walk, unable to climb steps, there was no question of him playing. The Lakers adjusted for the surprise offense that had defeated them in the second half of the fifth game and won the sixth easily, 135–113. Playing virtually unmolested, Chamberlain missed only seven shots. He scored 45 points.

Reed and the team's trainer, Danny Whelan, left Los Angeles immediately after the sixth game ended to return to New York and more treatment—heat, ice, whirlpool, massage. They worked together Thursday and then again Friday afternoon, the day of the last game. Holzman told writers, "It's up to the doctor if Willis plays in the seventh game. I'm not going to ask him because he'll say he's all right."

Reed told Whelan he would play in the game "if I have to crawl out there." Whelan believed him, but he also believed Holzman when he said he "would not risk Willis Reed's future for any championship." Reed had dozens of calls during the four days, days that seemed to race by. Fred Hobdy, his coach at Grambling, called. He wasn't a Knute Rockne; he didn't believe in orations. He simply told his former pupil, "You've got to be on the floor when they throw the ball up."

Reed called his mother before the game—she didn't feel there was an incongruity in addressing the Knicks' captain as

"Junior"—and then returned to his treatments in Whelan's room. The Knicks, dressing, had only one question they endlessly put to each other: "Will he go? Is he going to go?" But, of course, none of them had the answer.

Neither did Holzman nor Reed. Hours before the game was to start, Reed pulled on his uniform and warmup suit and went out into the deserted Garden to test his leg. His face was impassive as he moved slowly around the basket lofting in one-handed shots; he had noticed Chamberlain and Laker coach Joe Mullaney watching. When he returned to the Knicks' dressing room, his only comment to Whelan was "It hurts."

Holzman and Reed waited for the team doctor's decision. It came: Reed could play; although the muscle remained extremely painful, it had healed enough so there was no possibility of permanent injury. The rest of the team went into the arena to warm up as Reed remained behind to receive a pregame shot of cortisone and a painkiller.

With everyone but Reed on the court and DeBusschere standing in as captain for the pregame ritual with the officials and the Laker captain, the Garden was wild with anticipation.

Finally, a lone figure walked out slowly through the runway leading from the dressing rooms. Literally dragging his right leg behind him, Reed limped to the Knicks' bench. The Garden exploded with sound when the crowd saw him in uniform. The spectators shrieked louder as they saw him remove his warmup clothes to start the game. Reed never heard the ovation. He was thinking, "I have to play a man six inches taller than me and stronger than me, a man who had just had a 45-point game. I can't run and I can't jump and somehow I've got to compensate for all that." The Lakers watched Reed silently and seemed mesmerized.

Reed jumped center against Chamberlain, then moved downcourt, took a pass and put the game's first shot, a gentle one-hander from about 22 feet out, through the basket. It didn't even touch the rim. He was not only playing but in the opening seconds he had burned the Lakers.

The crowd was on its feet, screaming. Chamberlain scored for the Lakers, Bradley put in a foul shot for New York and then Reed took another pass with only 83 seconds gone and popped in a second one-hander. He had taken two shots and scored both times. The Knicks led, 5–2.

The Lakers were finished. The team that had won without difficulty two days earlier never threatened. Reed didn't score again—he took only three more shots—nor did he write any other impressive statistics in that game. But he gave his teammates an extraordinary emotional lift that carried them to a one-sided win that was more a rout than the final 113–99 score indicated.

And he kept Chamberlain away from the basket. Weakened, playing on nerve and pride, Reed was able to move Chamberlain and reduce his effectiveness immeasurably. He realized he had to force Chamberlain out a foot or two. When Chamberlain could simply turn around and drop the ball into the basket, he'd score on nine out of 10 shots. But if he could be forced to shoot from, perhaps, five or six feet instead of three, he would score 50 percent or, on a poor night, 40 percent. And then he would be just another player. He would no longer be Wilt Chamberlain, the devastating weapon.

The rest of the Knicks darted superbly around Reed. "The Lakers looked stunned," DeBusschere wrote. "They couldn't believe what we were doing to them."

Reed remained on the floor for about 20 minutes in the first half and seven in the second, not much more than half the game. But it was enough to bring the Knicks their first world championship.

Reed competed with an injury that defied painkilling drugs. The muscle he strained stretches from hip to knee and controls the movement of the leg. The injury was severe enough to make even walking painful. Reed, even with drugs that night, couldn't run. He just limped around the floor dragging his right leg, moving because he willed himself to move.

I can think of few athletes who would have made the effort he did. Not because they're not fine athletes or brave men willing to play hurt, but because his was an exceptional exhibition.

As Reed told me when I interviewed him immediately after the game for television, "I was going to go out there and play. All of my life was that one game. Waiting for me was the greatest center who ever played the game. I had an obligation to myself. And I had a responsibility. I had to help. The pain was there. It never left me. I couldn't run, I couldn't jump, I couldn't shoot, but I had to be there. People talk of choice. I *had* no choice."

The dressing room was pandemonium after the game. De-Busschere pushed through a mob of reporters around Reed and hollered, "Come here, Captain." Reed smiled, stood, and limped through the reporters to DeBusschere. Neither spoke; they just threw their arms around each other.

Cazzie Russell was to say at the Knicks' victory party, "The way he kept going, the way he kept moving Wilt, forcing him farther out, the captain showed me something. . . . He showed me he had more than guts. I don't know how he did it, but he got up and down the court and they weren't going to stop him unless a doctor came out there and got him."

Bradley, usually rather unemotional, told a writer, "He's always showing us new parts of himself. What dedication to the team."

Frazier, hero of the statistics with 36 points, said, "*He* was there and he is our leader . . . and we had to win it."

Wilt Chamberlain was the first Laker to go to the Knicks' dressing room after the game to congratulate them. He said simply, "It took a great deal of courage to do what he did."

Reed that year swept every honor in pro basketball: the Most Valuable Player in the league during the season, again for the playoffs and again for the All-Star game. He was also named to the first team All-NBA.

The muscle injury healed during the offseason but Reed, at the very peak of his success, would never be well again.

He began the next season, 1970–71, with tendonitis of the left knee so severe that only injections of cortisone enabled him to keep up with the Knicks' schedule. During one midseason period, the Knicks played 13 games in eight different cities within 20 days. "Reed played every game in that stretch," noted one reporter, "and because of the pride he takes in his work, played hard . . . so hard his teammates began to fear he would do himself permanent harm." Holzman shared that fear and benched Reed for five days.

He played the entire schedule in pain. He still averaged more than 20 points a game and pulled down more than 1,000 rebounds, but it was the last season he would do either. On a late-evening cab ride in Detroit in January 1971, a hurting, dispirited Reed told writer Bob Harding that the tendonitis was getting worse and might force him into premature retirement.

It did—10 months later. Playing with increasing pain, Reed finished the year. In May, his left knee was operated on. The surgery and the physical therapy that followed failed. Reed started the 1972–73 season and played only 11 games before he and physicians realized he couldn't continue.

When he left that game at halftime, he knew he would not return soon. "There's nothing I can compare with the feeling of frustration, helplessness, inability to contribute," he said. "After 11 regular-season games in 1971, I was standing there in the middle of the Garden and the realization was slowly coming on that I just wasn't of any help to the team. I had a tough time rebounding with the other centers. My moves toward the basket were not deceiving anyone. My quickness both on offense and defense was all but gone." The pain, even when he merely bent his knee to sit, was excruciating.

From that November 11, 1971, until October 21, 1972, Reed was not to play again. That year was to become the most difficult one in Reed's life. He was suddenly removed both from the sport he loved and the team he headed. In their place: a set of leg weights, a regimen of therapy, and a question—would he be able to play again? No doctor would promise that.

His left leg was put into an ankle-to-hip cast for six weeks to immobilize the knee. Then Reed began more stringent therapy to build up the knee and his atrophying muscles. The handicap of his left knee and the extreme weakness of that leg transformed him from one of the game's most agile and forceful big men into its biggest question mark. And *that* uncertainty changed one of the most approachable of superstars into a reserved, almost distant man. Normally warm and outgoing, Reed drew into himself. Everywhere he went, people asked about his knee, his future. He dreaded the questions and became somewhat of a recluse.

"I began to weave myself into such states of depression, such 'pits' that I never before knew existed," Reed was to say. "I began to lose interest in a great many things around me. I scratched for answers and came up empty and doubting. I became suspicious and worried and fearful."

Reed read about his teammates in the newspapers and kept exercising—day after endless day, three times a day, seven days a week. Would his career end this way, he wondered, with him on an exercise table all alone? The Knicks traded Cazzie Russell for center Jerry Lucas. Willis was in the last year of his contract.

"The team was winning without me," he said. "People

keep asking, 'Is Reed washed up?' The press wrote that I was, And all I could do was lecture myself over and over, 'You're the only one who got you out of Bernice, Louisiana, and you're the only one who can get you out of this problem.'"

Reed realized what so many professional athletes have learned. "When you're hurt, all the honors you've received don't count," he said. "I was the Most Valuable Player one year and not a member of the team the next. The world doesn't want to know what you did. It wants to know what you *will* do. No one is ever established. Every game is a new game and you have to prove yourself to the coach, the players, the fans. You have to prove every day that you are who your reputation says you are."

Just as he had driven himself to play basketball well enough so it would, at the least, bring him a college education, now he drove himself to get over his knee injury and return to the Knicks able to play again. Faced with a new crisis, he handled it the only way he knew, with work. "It was time," he said, "to see what I was made of."

For seven empty, lonely months, Reed worked to strengthen the left leg—and to see if the ever-present pain would diminish. Would he ever again bend a knee without pain? Would he put his 245 pounds on it without pain? Would he walk, run, jump? Would he play basketball again?

Gradually, the leg became stronger, the pain began to subside. By the start of the 1971–72 playoffs, his knee appeared healed, but Reed hadn't been able to work out since the start of the season. He was woefully out of condition. At about the time of the playoff finals, as Los Angeles was demolishing the Knicks in five games, as Wilt Chamberlain was outplaying the men standing in for Reed—DeBusschere and Lucas— Willis began to get back into shape, too late for that year, but there was a glimmer of hope for the next.

Reed sat out the first five games of the 1972–73 season. His knee, supported by a harness, felt good. But he wasn't the same player he had been. He never would be again. He had trouble cutting and racing on the fast break. He would have to pace himself more, use his experience to save steps. Although many writers picked New York to win the division title again, the team played inconsistently, good one night, ineffectively the next. Bradley, Frazier, and DeBusschere were the only starters who were healthy.

Reed would no longer play full-time. His scoring average fell almost by half. But he played a strong defense and was able to help work other members of the team free to shoot. The Knicks were still the smartest team in the league and that as much as anything else kept them in second place in the division.

The Knicks won the first two rounds of the 1972–73 playoffs, against Baltimore and Boston. Then it was the finals and the Lakers again.

It was a rematch of the 1969–70 playoffs when the Knicks with Reed defeated Los Angeles in seven games, and the 1971–72 playoffs when New York without Reed lost to Los Angeles in five.

This time the Knicks lost only one game to the club that had taken the championship from them the season before. Reed clearly was the difference. He returned to his pre-1971 form in two of the five games, playing most of the way in both, scoring 22 points in one and 21 in the second.

He was named Most Valuable Player in league playoffs a second time—another first in the NBA. Again Reed silenced the doubts and criticism that had risen during his absence. When the pressure was on, his skills and his "heart" were as strong as before.

He of course had no way of knowing, but his career essentially ended with his—and New York's—second championship. His other knee began to hurt badly at the start of the next season. He underwent surgery in mid-December and returned to the playoffs, but the Knicks were eliminated by Boston in the second round.

Reed's right knee was diagnosed as a degenerating form of arthritis, an ailment likely to cause permanent damage if he continued to play. He retired in summer 1974 after only 10 seasons, seven as a full-time athlete, six as a healthy one.

He had come back twice, in the seventh game of 1969–70 when his 27 minutes brought New York its first championship and 1972–73 when he led New York to its second, and most recent, title after a solitary year of rebuilding a leg. He had no such option where his right leg was concerned. Reed played center the way the position is supposed to be played. He had strength, competitiveness, quickness, and the ability to score. One or two of these is enough to make it as a pro and he had them all. Although he didn't play long enough to roll up great cumulative statistics, I think he was the best "small" center yet to play the game.

Willis and I sat recently in a room overlooking New York's Central Park and we talked of our own weaknesses in our respective sports. "I couldn't dribble," he recalled, smiling. "I couldn't jump as well as some, although timing helped make up some of the bounce I lacked. I wasn't as fast as I would have liked to have been."

He nodded in understanding as I discussed my earlier transition to a spectator's role after 12 years in pro football. Both of us lost a year in our professional careers because of injury. Both of us liked to play and miss it.

Reed says he has adjusted to the sidelines. "It's over. When I got that scholarship to Grambling, I never thought I would come this far. The most I dared hope for then was a teaching job, perhaps coaching, something to get me out of the fields."

I asked him how he'd like to be remembered by those who

saw him play. The answer came quickly. There were a "lot of things," he said, that he couldn't do to his satisfaction in basketball. "But what I could do, I did 100 percent. That's the only thing I'd like people to remember about me. What he could do, he *did*."

Ken
Venturi

They came into the public's consciousness together, Venturi and Palmer. They were both young, only two years apart. Hogan was king but aging and a crown prince was needed. To many insiders, golf's next decades would belong, not to Arnold Palmer, but to Ken Venturi.

For four years, Venturi was the favorite or co-favorite of every tournament he entered. In his first 19, he finished out of the money only once. His presence helped guarantee the success of any tour event. Businessmen competed to get his endorsement of their golf products.

Abruptly in 1961, at 29, Venturi disappeared from contention. Professionally and personally, his life fell apart. His game crumbled, his marriage disintegrated, his health collapsed, his money disappeared. But in one of the most moving stories I know in sports, he came back, not once but twice, as a golfer and, more importantly, as a man. His is the inspiring story of a defeated champion who refused to accept defeat.

Ken had reached the top so quickly: San Francisco city champion at 18—first of three times he would win that title—two-time California state amateur winner, member of the Walker Cup team at 21. When he was drafted into the army in 1953, it appeared just an interruption of an extraordinary career in the making.

Immediately after his discharge two years later, he was invited to play in the Masters. He had not qualified for it.

Former winners of the Masters—who had one invitation to give—asked him, primarily on the strength of Ken's victory over national amateur champion Harvie Ward in the San Francisco city competition. (Palmer had won the national amateur the previous year and immediately turned pro.)

Venturi came to Augusta, Georgia, site of the Masters, unbelievably sure of himself, unconcerned that at 24 he was about to play the full complement of golf's giants of that period. When he heard gossip that he was a dark horse favorite to win, Venturi was not surprised.

"I really thought I was going to win the Masters," Ken told me years later. "I wasn't brash; I was good and I knew it. I thought I was going to give that tournament a shot they'd remember." Near the first tee, Venturi noted the leaderboard, a large scoreboard of sorts that keeps spectators posted on hole-by-hole playing of the favorites. His name was not on that board but it took him just four holes to get it added.

He dropped a 20-foot putt on the first hole, followed with a six-foot putt on the second, a 21-footer on the third, and placed a 4-iron tee shot one foot from the cup on four, all for birdies. Suddenly, the gallery around Venturi and playing partner Billy Joe Patton swelled as spectators raced to see the unknown who had birdied the first four holes on the difficult Augusta National course.

Ken played the next eight holes in par. Patton twisted in a 35-foot putt on 13 for an eagle. Venturi jauntily approached his ball on 13. "Just step aside, Billy Joe, and I'll put mine right in on top of yours." He then drilled home a 25-foot putt for a duplicate eagle. He played par golf for the balance of the round for a 66, an 18-hole record for an amateur. That gave him a one-stroke lead over defending champion Cary Middlecoff.

Ken's next two rounds, 69 and 75 (setting a three-round record for an amateur), gave him a four-stroke lead going into final Sunday. Wind, which had begun to blow hard on the second day, increased to gusts of gale force during the third round. The best score of the day was 72. Middlecoff shot 75 to remain four behind Venturi. Jackie Burke, Venturi's third-round partner, carded 75 and ended the day eight strokes back.

Suddenly that evening, Ken began to realize where he was and what he was doing. Almost nauseated by a nervousness he had never felt before, Venturi approached the first tee for the final round as a spectator asked him, "How does it feel to be the first amateur to take the Masters?" If Ken won, he would also be the youngest Masters champion.

Two bogies on the front nine gave Ken 80—and second place. Burke scored 71 to edge Venturi by one stroke. Writers were to call that round, among other terms, a "stunning collapse." It wasn't that at all.

Ken hit no really bad shots, but he three-putted seven greens. Clearly, his nerve got to him. But the course that day demolished everyone's game. Wind gusts of 40 and 45 miles an hour, mixed with abrupt periods of deceptive calm, had players hesitating over selection of clubs. In the 220-yard fourth hole, for example, one where players normally would use a 2-iron or 3-iron, the wind was blowing from green to tee and even the long hitters were reaching for their drivers. The wind and the sun had made greens pavement hard. Putts that were barely tapped skipped yards past holes. Only Burke and Sam Snead broke par that day—by one stroke. Middlecoff scored 80. Burke's 289 remains the highest score ever to win the Masters.

But some spectators and writers, looking for the quick judgment, dismissed Venturi with "choker." It was a stupid label that took Ken eight years to live down.

Venturi flew home to find his troubles increasing. A wire-service reporter was at the airport with Venturi's family. Ken's mother was crying and, to comfort her, Venturi said, "Don't worry, Mom, we'll win the Open." The reporter asked Venturi why the Masters officials had changed the final-day pairings. It was traditional at that tournament for the leading golfer to play his final round with Byron Nelson. Because Venturi was Nelson's protégé, the officials felt his victory might be tainted if he were to win with Nelson at his side. Venturi agreed. "Who," they asked, "would you like to play with instead?"

Ken thought: *If I'm going to walk in as a winner, I want to do it with one of the all-time greats.* He asked to be paired with Snead. "Did Snead," the reporter in San Francisco asked, "talk to you during the round?" "No," replied Venturi and went on to say that Snead had tried but Ken was so nervous he couldn't talk; Snead thought it best to leave him alone.

In next morning's papers, the story read: (1) Venturi was furious and believes he lost the Masters because the pairings were changed; (2) Snead hurt him by giving him the silent treatment instead of support; (3) Venturi vows revenge on the Masters, pledges to win the Open.

Simultaneously, Ken was written off as a braggart and crybaby. It would be years before he would change people's minds.

Furious over this new reputation, Venturi abruptly decided to turn professional. He had intended to remain an amateur and gain his living by selling cars for Ed Lowery, a very close friend and member of the executive committee of the United States Golf Association. Purses on the pro tour then were small. Lowery had offered Ken an auto dealership in San Francisco that could, in time, make him a wealthy man.

But Venturi now had something to prove: He was neither afraid of pressure nor a crybaby.

Venturi had had to prove something to himself once before. Golf was the fortuitous by-product. Ken began playing golf when he was 14 because it was the best way he could figure out to get over a severe stammer. The impediment started when he was about nine, caused, his mother believed, when she tried to change him from left- to right-handed. By 12, Ken couldn't speak a full sentence. He was unable to recite in class. He refused to talk on the telephone. Therapists insisted he could speak if he wanted to. Pressure made the problem worse. Mimicked in class, Venturi's only response was to attack whoever was taunting him. Because bullies tease only those they can whip, Venturi's fights usually were futile affairs. His nose was cauterized several times in one semester.

Finally, Ken decided that only he could cure the stammer. To do it, he would have to be alone. An excellent athlete, he decided to try to combine his "home" therapy with a saving grace, sports. His father managed a public golf course, so Venturi went there after school each day, all day on weekends and vacations. For four lonely years he taught himself to speak—and, almost as an afterthought, to play golf.

Alone on a deserted section of the course he would talk to a phantom gallery, explain at length the shots he was making, offer gracious acceptance speeches for "winning" the Open, the Masters, the PGA, every golf tournament of significance in the world. Slowly, as the teenager worked out his speech problems, his self-taught golf also took. By the time he was 17, his attention to his speech and to golf had paid off.

Suddenly, the kid who effectively had been ostracized through most of his school years—as much by his own determination to repair his problem as by the action of peers —found himself in demand. Golf, Venturi then realized, could allow him "to become somebody." He had reached his first goal. He had proved that he *alone* could repair his speech problem when the experts could not. Speech impediment corrected, he now determined to be the best golfer in the world.

Venturi turned pro in November 1956. Under the rules

then, he had to wait six months before he could compete for official prize money. That left him less than four months on the tour, but enough to be voted pro golf's Rookie of the Year. The following season opened with back-to-back wins. (Venturi had a firm sense of himself. When a friend expressed glee at the tour-opening victories, Ken said simply, "I wasn't surprised. I expected it.") Ken placed in every tournament he entered, winning seven. He earned $40,000 in official prize money during his first 16 months on the tour. In four years, he won $122,000, second high for that period of time. On the 1958 and 1960 tours only Palmer earned more money.

Analysts seemed to compete with each other in describing the fluid, classic way Venturi played. One: "Ken stands up to the ball as if he, the club, the ball, and the golf course were all part of a beautiful piece of sculpture." Another: "[He is] the finest iron player I have ever seen, not excepting Byron Nelson. . . ." From Nelson himself: "Ken's a thinker. Like Snead, Hogan, and myself, he's not only interested in shooting a low score, but in why he shoots a low score. He has a talent for saving strokes. I think he will take very few double bogies."

Nelson, an old friend of Lowery, had been introduced by Lowery to Ken in 1952. They played a round together and the comments that followed are part of golf legend: Venturi, after shooting a 66, "How was that, Mr. Nelson?" From Nelson, laconically but not unkindly, "I'm going to be here three more days. Meet me at nine o'clock tomorrow. There are seven or eight things we can fix in your swing that might make you a good player."

Nelson "took a nice piece of furniture and polished it almost beyond recognition," Venturi recalled later. "He taught me how to play." Ken had a powerful pair of hands and placed the burden of his swing on them. Nelson gave Venturi a new swing, joining hands, shoulder, and body into a balanced one-piece movement.

Nelson returned about six weeks later to play a series of exhibitions with Venturi. After each round, they talked. They went over the round hole by hole. "Why did you play that high approach shot on four?" Nelson would ask. "Do you think it might have come off better if you skipped it in low? Why did you lay up short on your second shot on 12 rather than go for the pin?" Nelson would explain why he would have played differently, if there was a diverging view, and always listened to Venturi's reasons for his choice of play.

Nelson and Venturi would spend almost as much time talking as playing. "The pin's in the back," Nelson might say, "and you have a full 9-iron or a ¾ 8-iron. But if you use the full 9-iron and nip it too much, the ball will hit short and back up. If you try to hit it hard, you might be over the green. What if you use the 8-iron, choke it down and skip the ball up, make it hop forward to the pin? If the pin were in the front of the green, what about using a 9-iron hard and dropping it behind the pin?" Venturi took notes during the lessons, exhibitions, and conversations and kept them. He frequently referred to them in later years.

Ken was young and successful and cocky. During a practice round for his first official tournament at Flint, Michigan, Venturi hit his second shot, a wedge, into the hole for an eagle. On the next hole, also a par four, his tee shot carried to within 90 yards of the green. As Venturi walked down the fairway, a spectator commented, "Boy, that was a lucky shot at the last hole." "Lucky, hell," said Venturi. "Watch this." He drilled his second shot 90 yards into the hole for another eagle.

Although Ken's success on the tour was immediate and emphatic, the Masters came back twice more to wound him deeply. The 1958 Masters was a special "moment" for both Venturi and Palmer. As the leading money winner on the tour going into the 1958 Masters, Ken was the choice of most to win the Masters that year. Both men were in the dawn of their careers. Both were looking for that first major win—

an Open, a PGA, a Masters. And, as it turned out, both took sharply divergent paths after that tournament. Palmer of course became the personification of an era in the sport. Venturi? His future consisted of brilliant flashes of what might have been.

The "choking" label cropped up continually. Venturi shot 68 in the first round to take the lead. He fired 40 for the first half of the second round and, as he was walking to the 10th tee, heard someone say, "There he goes, choking again." Furious, Venturi shot 32 on the back nine—four birdies and five pars—to keep the lead.

Venturi and Palmer were paired together in the final round. They were tied going into the 155-yard par three 12th. Arnie's drive carried over a creek past the green and bounded up to a mound short of a trap. Ken's tee shot held the back edge of the green. Palmer's ball was imbedded in the side of the mound and officials at first ruled he could not get a free lift.

After Venturi holed out for a par, Palmer hit his second shot about two feet into rain water at the base of the mound, chipped to the green and two-putted for a five. That returned Venturi to the lead by two. Palmer also played a second, or provisional, ball. He took a free lift, chipped close to the pin and dropped his putt for a three. A five was posted for Palmer on the giant leaderboard.

Arnie then hit a marvelous approach to the par-five 13th and holed that putt for an eagle. Venturi scored a birdie to lead by one. When Palmer and Venturi were approaching the 14th green, the ruling for the 12th hole was reversed. Palmer was given a three. That returned him to the lead over Venturi by one stroke. Angry, rattled, Venturi three-putted the 14th, to fall two behind Palmer. Both men parred the remaining holes and Palmer won his first green jacket. Doug Ford and Fred Hawkins, the only other challengers, both missed birdie putts on the last green that would have tied them with Palmer.

At the 1960 Masters, Venturi took the lead from Palmer in the last round. As Arnie began the last three holes, needing a par and two birdies to defeat Venturi, Ken was brought into the press room to be interviewed by writers, the apparent winner.

Shooting from about 40 feet out on the 16th green for a birdie, Arnie put too much on the ball, but his shot hit the pin and bounced back three feet. Palmer dropped the putt for a par three. If the shot had not hit the pin, it might have gone over the green, possibly into a trap on the far side. Palmer then pulled off successive birdies—he dropped a 45-foot putt on 17 and an eight-foot putt on 18—for the stroke he needed to defeat Venturi.

Ken didn't know it, but his career had crested and a long, agonizing slide had begun. The reason? One can only speculate. Hogan terms golf: "20 percent technique, 80 percent mental." So it is and who, including Ken, can point with authority and say, "There, that's when it began"?

Venturi himself blames his 1960 Masters loss when Palmer birdied the last two holes to beat him. He further questioned his fate at the 1961 Masters when Arnie double-bogied the same 18th hole to allow Gary Player to win by one stroke.

Venturi had been within a total of four strokes of winning three Masters titles, yet there was nothing to show for his effort (only Snead had won three Masters to that point).

What about taking pride in being second? "What is second?" Ken was to respond scornfully. "Second is nothing. Second is a loser. I don't hang second places on my wall."

Ken began to feel sorry for himself. "Call it self-pity if you will," he told me, "because that's what it was." For the first time in his career Venturi failed to qualify for the Open (he would miss again in 1962 and 1963). His good health began to desert him. He contracted walking pneumonia, remained on the tour with it for four months before it was diagnosed, and then reacted violently to the antibiotic prescribed.

His marriage, rocky for several years, worsened. Venturi's marital problems lasted through the sixties. He and his wife, whom he had married in 1953 and with whom he had had two sons, separated stormily a number of times, finally for good in 1970.

In Palm Springs in 1962, a sudden, piercing pain through his chest and back forced him to his knees at the 11th tee of the third round. He finished the round; a 68, thanks to a 31 on the front nine, kept him in contention. He tried to play the final day but, unable to swing a club, dropped out. His physician believed the pain was due to a pinched nerve and advised several months of rest. Venturi refused to leave the tour. His pain worsened. It was months before he could even reach his right hand to his head. Trying to favor his back, he shortened and flattened his swing. His game began to deteriorate. At one tournament, he shot 80 in the opening round and was so embarrassed that he withdrew.

Ken became plagued by misgivings and anger. His buoyant self-confidence disappeared. He began to drink more than he should.

The back spasms continued through 1962 and most of 1963. Venturi played as much as possible. There were flashes of brilliance following the 1960 Masters, but the shadow of that loss remained with him. In the Texas Open in 1962, he drove a tee shot in the first round into an earth fissure, a crack caused by extreme heat and dryness. Because the policy in past years there had been to take a free drop when that happened, Venturi automatically took the lift and continued to play.

In the final round, five under par and within one stroke of

the lead, Ken heard someone mention that a free lift out of a fissure was not allowed that year because officials had forgotten to include that ruling on the rule sheet. Taking a drop meant a one-shot penalty. Venturi had signed his card with a wrong total for the first round. Ken picked up his ball and disqualified himself. Elated until then, "suddenly, like a pricked balloon, all of my new-found hope was blotted out." Raging at his luck, he went home.

He developed tendonitis in his left wrist from making adjustments in his swing. In a televised rematch of a duel pitting Nelson and himself against Palmer and Player—Nelson and Venturi had won the year before—Ken was humiliated by his performance.

Ken began to lose control over the things that mattered most to him—his family and his golf. "I was a shambles mentally," he told me years later. "I knew my ability. I knew how far I *could* go—but I couldn't win a tournament, I couldn't make a cut. So maybe I wasn't as good as I thought I was." 1962 and 1963 became lost years. His winnings fell to $6,951 in 1962 and to $3,848 in 1963. "I was playing poorly, thinking unsoundly and continually in a bad frame of mind."

Although he had never stopped practicing, now he found reasons to avoid that. He spent more time drinking to hide the reality of his present. Always quick-tempered, his drinking made him belligerent.

A casual acquaintance slapped him on the shoulder one night in a bar.

Venturi spun around. "Don't hit me," he snapped.

"Anybody can touch you, Venturi," the man replied. "You're a has-been."

Venturi leaped at the man and knocked him to the floor.

Ken disappeared for days at a time. Everywhere he went, he heard—or imagined—whispers: "Venturi's through." Ed

Lowery tried to help, but Venturi wouldn't listen to him. Nelson invited Venturi to visit his ranch home in Texas. Venturi refused. Byron called again and persisted. Venturi spent a week with Nelson and his wife, Louise, both of whom he liked enormously. But his defenses were so high, no one could reach him.

Invited to the Sahara Invitational in Las Vegas in 1963, he arrived at the tournament to be told, in a room filled with other golfers and hangers-on, that his name wasn't on the list of players. A clerical error. But all the spots had been filled. He was turned away. He went back to the motel to pack. "Not only did I believe I wasn't any good, but I was convinced no one else thought I was either."

Before he could check out of his motel, four pros—Gardner Dickinson, Jay and Lionel Hebert, and Mike Souchak—told the tournament director that either Venturi receive an invitation or they were dropping out. They forced the director to ask Venturi to play. Wounded, Ken refused. But his friends persuaded him to change his mind. "I didn't want to play. All of the pros knew I wasn't on the invitation list. But I had enough belief in my ability that I stayed." Venturi, who had earned money in only eight tournaments that year, never finishing higher than 18th, won $675.

Ken now was reduced to asking tournament directors for exemptions, permission to play without having to qualify in pretournament matches with the "rabbits," golfers on the fringe of the circuit who have to earn the right to play tournament by tournament. Top money winners earn exemptions by virtue of their performance. After three years of losing, Venturi had no more exemptions. He was too proud to play with the rabbits—and perhaps afraid that he couldn't qualify.

"I would rather have gone 15 rounds with Marciano than play a round of tournament golf then, but I kept going. I had to. I didn't know what else to do." Ken didn't always get the exemptions he requested. During the good years, 1956 through 1960, invitations had flowed in to him. Tournament directors *had* to have Venturi. Once the slide began, Ken learned the way of the world where yesterday's heroes are concerned.

Always highstrung, Venturi's nerves were unremittingly on edge. Overhearing a conversation one day that appeared to indicate a close friend had given up on him, Venturi headed straight for a bar. Sitting there, alone and tearful at closing time, Ken noticed the owner looking at him. He had known the man for years. "Venturi, you're a mess," the man said. "You had everything, you're still young, yet you sit here like a damned bum."

Ken was virtually broke. His product endorsements, a rich source of money for winning pros, were running out and not being renewed. He had enough money for one more round on the circuit. But his game had disintegrated.

Somewhere, Venturi found the inner resources to drive himself back to practice. Day after day, seven days a week, six or seven hours a day, he would work alone—in a ritual reminiscent of a 14-year-old boy determined to cure a speech impediment. Now, Venturi was trying to salvage his self-esteem. (Years later, I asked him if he was driven to prove to his critics that he could once again play championship golf. "No," he replied. "I was trying to prove it to myself.")

But he *was* driven. In the manner of Hogan who had once said, "There isn't enough daylight in any day to practice all the shots you need to," Venturi broke his game down to its basic components and started to rebuild it. He pulled out the notes he had made with Nelson and studied them. He worked on one club at a time, for hours, often days. He spent one three-day period on his 6-iron. And at the end of each long day, however tired, he would hit 100 more tee shots. No matter if he had been working on tee shots all day, he would stand there and hit 100 more.

Somewhere in his early years, perhaps while he was battling the cruelties of mimicry in school or as he passed four years taming a stutter on an empty golf course, Ken learned to be comfortable alone. More, he realized early that in the final analysis each of us has only ourselves. So when he got into deep trouble, he turned away even from friends such as Lowery and Nelson and resolved to do what he could alone. It had to be his way.

He was criticized for "aloofness." "I admit I'm a loner," he told one writer, "and what I do I have to do by myself. When I'm on the course, I find the only way I can relax is to keep my mind completely on the game. When I talk to people, I lose my concentration; and then if I hit a bad shot or a stupid shot, I get furious at myself for breaking my trend of thought. Other people, like Lee Trevino, relax when they have someone to talk to. If I see someone in the gallery and just barely nod to them, people think I'm standoffish. But a slight nod from me is exactly like Lee going over and giving them a big slap on the back."

Slowly, as he tried to work his game back into form quietly, not complaining, many of those who had turned away from him in disgust during his golden years became staunch supporters. "I'll never forget," says pro Dave Marr, "how he sat with all of us through dinner one night after missing the cut at a tournament and never once talked about a shot or mentioned his bad luck. That was class."

It was 1964 and another tour was beginning. Venturi tentatively ventured into several tournaments. First, the Los Angeles Open. He usually played well here. He missed the cut for the final 36 holes by one stroke.

Venturi went to see an old friend, Bill Varni, who owned a restaurant in San Francsico.

"I just don't think I'm going to make it back," Ken saia.

Varni became angry. "You just bet you're going to make it," he said. "I have a hunch this is going to be the greatest year you've ever had."

Venturi smiled sadly. "That's pretty far-fetched."

"All you need is four or five more tournaments," Varni said. "I'll make you a deal. I'll write you a check for $50,000 right now if you'll agree to give me everything you win or endorse this year. Keep your past contracts, but give me your winnings and bonuses and I'll give you $50,000."

Venturi refused because he didn't want to take advantage of a friend. But buoyed by Varni's confidence, Venturi entered the Bing Crosby and Palm Springs tournaments—and again failed to make the cuts. He continued to practice. He won $295 in the Lucky International in San Francisco and picked up two more small, but needed, checks at Pensacola and St. Petersburg.

Once again the Masters intruded. Ken had become convinced that a comeback, if there was to be one, would start at Augusta. He hadn't qualified for the Masters that year, but believed he would be given an invitation for his past performances (he had played in every Masters since leaving the army in 1955). For weeks, he called home daily from stops along the tour to ask if the invitation had come. It never did. In Greensboro, North Carolina, a local newspaper reported the Masters entrants. Venturi was not among them.

It was an extraordinary blow to his pride. In four years, he had slipped from the man who had almost won the Masters three times to the man no one wanted there. "That was the killer," he said. "I'd come to believe that I'd always be invited to the Masters." (The Masters that year was won by Palmer, his fourth triumph there since he and Ken had battled head to head during the final round in 1958.) Crushed, Venturi precipitously pulled out of the Greensboro competition and flew home.

Several weeks later, he tried again, this time the Houston and

Texas Opens. He didn't place in either, but now, for the first time since 1960, Ken believed his game was coming back. He returned home to prepare for the Oklahoma City Open and the start of the summer tour. While home, he began to spend time with a priest he knew, the Rev. Francis Murray. The pair spent several long evenings together. Venturi found comfort in the support the young clergyman offered him.

He again failed to place among the money winners at Oklahoma City and at Memphis, but Venturi was now sustaining himself. He felt his game increasingly improve; absence of a check didn't alter his conviction. Most important, the week following the Memphis tournament, he shot 67–70 to become the third low qualifier in the first of two qualifying trials for the 1964 Open.

Indianapolis followed and if Venturi made the final cut there, he would gain entry to the rich purse at the following week's Thunderbird Tournament in New York. He missed the Indianapolis cut by one stroke. Months earlier, that defeat would have sent him reeling home. Now he called Bill Jennings, director of the Thunderbird, and pleaded for a sponsor's invitation to the competition. He told Jennings the truth: He was broke and couldn't afford to fly to New York if he wasn't sure of getting into the tournament. "If I go home now, I'll never be back on the tour. You've got to help me."

"Sure I swallowed my pride," Ken said, "but I had finally learned a man can swallow his pride when he believes in himself. I knew my game was coming."

Jennings was equally candid. As kindly as possible, he told Venturi only one sponsor's invitation remained and Ken wasn't qualified for it on the basis of his current performance. He asked Venturi to call him back the next day. ("If Jennings had said, 'I'm sorry, Ken, but we're going to give it to John Jones because you shot 80 in the first round last year and withdrew,'" Ken told me, "I wouldn't have disliked him because he would have done what he believed to be the right thing.") The next day, Venturi received that last invitation.

While Tony Lema and Souchak battled for first place during the final round of the Thunderbird, Venturi found himself in the middle of a tangle of pros trying to get a lock on third place. The 16th hole, a tricky par three, was critical. The distance to the green demanded a 3-iron, but Ken knew that if he missed the green to either side, he could conceivably take a double- or triple-bogey six in recovering. The safe way would have been to use a 4-iron, put the ball just short of the green where there were no hazards, and then chip to the green and hopefully putt in for a par or, at worst, a bogey that may have been sufficient to insure third place.

Earlier in '64, he had been backing off from shots because he was afraid. He didn't have the confidence to take the chances often necessary to win. "But I told myself then that if I back off again, I would back off for the rest of my life." Ken took his 3-iron and put the ball down right on the green. He two-putted for par. Venturi went on to birdie 17, par 18, and finish in a tie for third. It was worth $6,250.

He then raced to Franklin Hills near Detroit for the second qualifying round for the Open. He shot 77–70 to qualify by three shots. The Buick Open in Grand Blanc, Michigan, was three days later. Venturi gained sixth place there—$3,200, which, added to the Thunderbird winnings, brought him more tour money in two weeks than in the prior two years.

The Open was next, the most important annual test in American golf, scheduled for the Congressional Country Club in Washington, D.C., at 7,053 yards the longest course in Open history. Washington in an average summer is no place to be, but the '64 Open came in the middle of an extraordinary spell of heat and humidity.

The favorites were Palmer and Jack Nicklaus. No one thought Ken a challenge; not even Venturi's caddy, clearly unhappy over whom he had drawn. When you make your living carrying a golf bag, you don't look for probable losers; they don't give bonuses. The caddy, however, approached his job seriously. To be of maximum help to the man he was to carry for, the caddy had taken a tape measure to the course and knew yardages almost to the inch. To Ken, who had never played the Congressional and knew he wouldn't be able to get in many practice holes in that oppressive heat and humidity, this was extremely valuable. "I can't promise you that I'm going to win this tournament," Venturi told his caddy, William Ward, father of seven children, "but I can tell you that if I do, I'll give you a thousand dollars."

The night before competition began, Ken went to church. He didn't ask to win, rather "Please let me believe in myself. . . . Dear God, I know my game has returned and all I ask is that you won't let me lose confidence in myself."

Venturi shot a 38–34—72 in the first round, two over par. Palmer's 68 was low. On Friday, Venturi shaved two strokes off his round with 70, but a young pro, Tommy Jacobs, tied what was then the all-time low for a round in an Open with 64. Jacobs now led Palmer, 136 to 137. Ken was six strokes back. On the way out of the clubhouse, he stopped for his mail. There was a six-page letter from Father Murray. It read, in part:

> Dear Ken:
> For you to become the 1964 U.S. Open champion would be one of the greatest things that happened during the year. . . .
> There are so many people who need the inspiration and encouragement that your winning would give them.
> Most people are in the midst of struggle. If not with their jobs, then it's their family life or their health or their drinking or their frustrations. For many, there is the constant temptation to give up and to quit trying.

Life seems to be too much and the demands are too great.

If you would win the Open, you would prove to millions of people that they can be victorious over doubt and struggle and frustration and despair. . . .

(You will need) faith in yourself. This you have in more than enough measure. . . . You are at peace within yourself. . . . You respect yourself. You are a new Ken Venturi. . . . now wise and mature and battle-toughened. You are more philosophical and self-controlled, more calm, more resourceful, more determined, more realistic.

The letter brought Ken an extra measure of serenity. "I wasn't thinking of winning the Open," he was to say later about the morning of the final 36 holes on Saturday. "I was thinking of finishing in the top 16 and automatically getting a spot in the 1965 Open without having to qualify. I was tranquil, very calm for some reason. I'd always been jumping just before a match, ready to explode at the first tee. Not that day."

Palmer and Jacobs were paired head to head for the final two rounds and the gallery of course was with them. Venturi's partner was Ray Floyd, a talented young pro. Venturi and Floyd teed off for the first 18 holes at 8:30. The temperature was already above 90°. It would rise to 104° by noon. The humidity at 8:30 was 96 percent. Ken and Ray went off virtually unnoticed about two groups ahead of the leaders.

Superstitious, as many athletes are, Ken found an omen at the first hole. A perfect drive and approach shot brought him to within 10 feet of the pin. The putt ran right up to the hole—and dangled on the lip. Finally, as Venturi began to walk toward it, the ball fell in for a birdie. *That could have hung outside,* Venturi thought, *and now I have one shot to play with. If I lose it, I'll become conservative.*

The next eight holes brought a gallery. He birdied the

fourth, fifth, eighth and ninth holes. He shot par on the remaining holes for a front-nine 30, matching the record for nine holes in an Open. He passed Palmer—who was missing greens and had bogied the first three holes—and Jacobs briefly at nine, but Venturi never glanced at the leaderboard and so didn't know it.

"I wasn't thinking of anyone during the first nine holes," Ken told me the next day. "Palmer never entered my mind. Nobody did. My game had returned to the way I used to play. That was the important thing. I was within myself. No one else mattered on the golf course."

Venturi's iron play, always his strongest game, had returned in such remarkable fashion that he had had at least two chances to lower that 30. He missed possible close-in putts for birdies on the third and seventh greens.

"It didn't hit me until I finished the first nine that I had a chance to win. I had no idea what was happening on the course elsewhere, but at the end of nine I thought I couldn't be more than a couple of shots behind." At that point, Ken consciously put himself into a shell of concentration that he would not break until the end of the day.

He parred the 10th and 11th holes and then hit a superb 4-iron shot on the par-3 188-yard 12th hole that stopped about 10 feet to the left of the pin. He played the putt to break down about four inches and it ran right into the middle of the cup. He birdied the 13th, parred the next three. On 17, his second shot hit the green about 15 feet from the hole. If he made the putt for a birdie, he would go seven under par.

Now the weather, which had begun to affect Venturi on the 15th hole, caused him to begin trembling as if he were palsied. Ken had eaten very little for breakfast. Unused to playing in the kind of heat and humidity in which he now found himself, he had taken little liquid and no salt tablets. Venturi was becoming dehydrated. He was having difficulty breathing and walking and, soon, even standing as vertigo hit him.

His putt on 17 ran about 18 inches short and as Ken bent over the ball, his vision blurred. He missed to end with a bogey. Now shaking uncontrollably, he bogied 18 as well. Nonetheless, his 30–36–66 put his three-round total at 208, in second place, two strokes behind Jacobs who had pulled up to a 34 during the second half of his morning round.

Ken's friend and fellow pro Jay Hebert saw him walk off the 18th green, helped him into a car, and drove with him up the hill to the clubhouse. Venturi failed to recognize Hebert. Jay was to tell Venturi later that his eyes kept rolling up under his lids, he was deathly white, and could barely stand. He was suffering from heat prostration.

A physician and member of the Congressional Country Club, John Everett, was called into the locker room from the gallery. Ken had 50 minutes until he had to tee off for the second round. Dr. Everett began feeding him repeated glasses of iced tea and salt tablets.

When the call came for Venturi to return to the course, Dr. Everett put a hand on his arm. "Don't go back out there," he said. "If you try to play again in this heat and in your condition, it could kill you."

"Dr. Everett, this may very well be my last shot," Ken said. "I have to finish this, no matter what the consequences."

"You could easily go into convulsions," the physician replied. "The Red Cross has had several cases here already among the spectators."

When Dr. Everett realized that Ken intended to play, he obtained permission to walk with him carrying an ice bag, cold towels, and a hypodermic filled with medication should Venturi convulse. When Venturi saw the hypodermic, he drew the physician to a corner of the locker room. "I want you to promise me something," he said. "Unless I collapse, don't use that needle. Don't count me out. I'll sign anything you want to take the responsibility from you, but please do as I ask." Dr. Everett agreed.

Venturi, playing slowly, parred seven of the first eight holes. Jacobs double-bogied the par-3 second hole and Venturi, again, was tied with him briefly for the lead. Palmer birdied the first hole, giving his supporters hope that he might make another of the rallying finishes that he had become famous for, and which had defeated Ken in the 1960 Masters. But Arnie bogied the next two and fell back to stay.

Venturi and Jacobs remained even until Ken reached the ninth, a 599-yard par 5 with a 40-yard ravine splitting the fairway just short of the green. Venturi's tee shot and 1-iron, the latter hit boldly and perfectly to bring the ball within just 10 yards of the ravine, gave him a chance to get a birdie four. The pin was placed far back in the green with a sand trap only 20 feet behind it. Rather than play safe and hit short to get on the green front and avoid the trap, Venturi went for the pin. His wedge shot stopped just eight feet behind the cup. His downhill putt requiring a big break to the left was perfect. Ken's birdie put him into the lead by one. He would remain there.

"Becoming ill was a blessing in disguise for me," he told me later. "When I reached the last holes, I was so sick and so tired that I really thought I was going to die. My eyes felt as if someone had their fingers in them. I don't remember how I kept walking. All I saw as I walked was the flag, each one in turn the size of a telephone pole. All I felt was I've got to go from this tee to that pin and from that pin to that tee. I never saw the creeks or the trees or the people behind the flags. I heard them applauding but as from a distance, softly, muffled. My reflexes took over. Those endless days of practicing, of working on each club, on every conceivable variety of shots with each club, had programmed me. My illness, my fatigue eliminated all pressure. I never had a chance to tighten up. I never realized what I had done—or exactly how I had done it—until I saw the films weeks later."

Venturi fought for each step and each breath. He felt as if he were in some sort of grotesque dance in which he and the golf course were continually moving toward and then away from each other. He recalled thinking that he was working like a machine, in slow motion to be sure, but a machine nonetheless.

He bogied one hole on the front nine when a short putt died at the edge of the cup.

"Tough luck," he heard someone comment.

Venturi heard himself replying, "They'll go down in time. They always do. It's a patient game."

When Ken reached 14, Dr. Everett, walking beside him all the way, gave him more iced tea and several more salt tablets. Ken was now leading by five; he had made up an incredible seven strokes. But all he was thinking was *I wonder how many people are asking if Venturi is going to fold again.*

Ken asked his caddy for a 6-iron at the 14th tee. "No," his caddy told him. "It's a 5-iron shot."

Venturi thought he could reach the green with the 6-iron. That was the only club he was to miss on all day. It fell short by about a foot of carrying over a deep bunker in front of the green. He blasted out and had to settle for a bogey, which put him back at par and reduced his lead to four strokes. He parred the 15th and hit his finest shot of the Open at the 16th tee, a 1-iron that missed hitting the pin by about two inches and rolled 12 feet past the hole. He parred that hole and the next in spite of catching the rough with his tee shot on 17.

Finally, he reached 18, the last hole, a long par-4 sloping gradually down to the green. He could take a seven and still win. He hit his drive and ahead of him saw a friend, Bill

Hoelle, put his arms straight over his head to signify the ball was in the center of the fairway. For the first time that day, Venturi went over to talk to someone. He walked to Hoelle and said, "Bill, how do we stand?"

"Just stay on your feet, Ken," Hoelle replied, "you've got it won."

A player can't see the green on Congressional's 18th until he gets about 125 yards from the tee. Water was to the left of the green. Venturi pushed his 4-iron approach to the right but too far and went into a bunker about 40 yards from the cup. (At about the same time the ball hit the sand trap, a fist fight broke out several yards away right on the fairway between two marshals vying for a better view. It was a vicious, noisy brawl. The fight itself didn't register with Ken. He dimly perceived two men rolling around and wondered what the devil they were doing. His only thought was *I hope those guys don't roll on my ball.*) Very slowly, Venturi began to follow his second shot. Joe Dey, executive secretary of the United States Golf Association, was nearby, occasionally slipping an arm under Venturi's when he thought it necessary. Venturi's face now was ashen. His eyes were glazed. He was shuffling and wobbling visibly.

He turned to Dey. "Joe, I'm sorry, but I've got to play slowly."

"It's downhill all the way to the green, Ken," Dey replied. "Just hold your chin up like a champion."

Venturi began the long walk down the sloping fairway, packed with people five- and six-deep along both sides. They were cheering and applauding him wildly. Venturi was somewhat startled. He had never had a gallery of yellers; it was always very proper applause. But now they were screaming and clapping. About 160 yards from the green, Venturi took off his cap and the entire gallery, an estimated 25,000 people, began to stand as he passed, as if the flag were parading by.

("I shall never forget the expression on his face as he came down the hill," writer Herbert Warren Wind was to note. "It was taut with fatigue and yet . . . radiant with pride and happiness.") The gallery cheered and applauded from the time Venturi crested the hill and started coming down until he was finished. They stopped briefly to allow him to blast out of the trap, a beautiful shot that landed 10 feet from the hole. Then they resumed. He pulled out his putter and they stopped. He sank the putt and they went wild. On that incredible afternoon, Ken shot 70.

Venturi dropped his putter. Twenty-one-year-old Ray Floyd, who was in junior high school when Venturi's career began to shatter, walked over to the hole, picked up Ken's ball, and handed it to him. He was crying. And, then, so was Ken.

Sweat mingled with tears as Venturi walked slowly off the 18th green. He was sweating of course long before the 18th. But, coming down that hill, hat off, to a gallery he had been waiting for since 1956, the tears may have started before he reached the green.

When he sat down minutes later to sign his scorecard, Ken kept staring at it, unable through his fatigue and illness to read it clearly, afraid to sign for fear it had been filled out wrong and he would disqualify himself. He kept repeating, "I don't remember the holes." Finally, Dey leaned over and said, "Ken, sign it. The score is right." Venturi looked up, recognized Dey, and signed the card. He finished with 278; only one man before him had ever won an Open with a lower score, Hogan with 276 in 1948.

Venturi's money problems were solved. His income following the Open victory jumped to almost $200,000, slightly over $76,000 from tour winnings (he finished the year in sixth place among touring pros), the balance from product endorsements, guest appearances, and exhibitions.

Ken quickly proved that the Open victory was no fluke. He won first money in the Insurance City Open, then placed fourth in the PGA, three strokes behind Bobby Nichols, the winner, and two back of Palmer and Nicklaus who were tied for second.

The American Golf Classic, played over one of the toughest courses on the tour, the Firestone Country Club in Akron, Ohio, was next. Ken shot 72–66–68–69—275 to win by five strokes over virtually the same field that had played in the Open. Mason Rudolph was second, Palmer, third, and Nick-laus, fourth. Venturi's score set a tournament record. He was the first man in the event's history to shoot three rounds in the 60s. He bogied only five holes.

Suddenly, everyone wanted Venturi: tournaments, appearances, endorsements, banquets. When he walked into Toots Shor's restaurant for lunch everyone stood and applauded him. He went to see *Hello, Dolly,* then running on Broadway, and as star Carol Channing danced out on a runway built into the audience, she stopped, grinned at Venturi, and pointed to him as she sang, "It's so good to have you back where you belong." Venturi and Miss Channing did not know each other.

Ken was to sweep every major golfing award that year: PGA Player of the Year, voted by the pros; the Ben Hogan Trophy, awarded annually to the golfer who overcomes physical handicap and continues to play; the Comeback of the Year; Sportsman of the Year, voted by *Sports Illustrated* magazine.

Most important, Ken's old skills had returned. He didn't need his showing in the Open, the PGA, Hartford, and the American Golf Classic to confirm it. Only 33, he believed he was back to stay.

But his game lasted less than six months.

In November, Venturi was paired against Player in the

Piccadilly World Match Play Championship in Wentworth, England. The weather was cold and rainy. Ken and Gary were even at the end of 31 holes. Venturi then topped iron shots on successive holes but attributed it to the biting cold wind. On the last four holes, as he lost 2 and 1, Venturi noticed that his fingers were blistered and had begun to peel. He dismissed it.

Playing in the Mexican Open the following month, the fingers were still blistered, swollen, and peeling. Now the tips were beginning to turn white whenever the hands were chilled and Ken began to lose feeling in them. He saw several doctors. None could diagnose the problem, but none thought it anything to be concerned about. Playing in Las Vegas during a rare snowstorm, his right hand began to hurt. Again, Venturi visited physicians. They had no diagnosis. Each said the problem would disappear.

The pain increased almost daily. Venturi's powerful hands began to weaken. "When I tried to play, it didn't feel as if I had a golf club in my hands. When I hit the ball, I never felt any sensation of impact." He had to test hot water with his forearm or elbow before washing his hands or he could have scalded himself.

Finally Venturi found a doctor who said the problem might be something called Raynaud's Phenomenon, a circulatory disorder that at worst, he said, could lead to gangrene in the fingers and amputation. He put Venturi on a heavy regimen of cortisone. By now, Ken's game had crumbled again. In cold weather, he lost all feeling in his hands. He had trouble closing his fingers around a club.

He picked up the tour at Pensacola, Florida, but there and in the events to follow, he was unable even to finish the opening rounds. When he took a golf club up and back, he had absolutely no idea where it was. He began to drop things constantly, a golf ball, a knife, a fork. He began squeezing sponges, hoping that might restore strength to his hands. They strengthened his forearms but his hands grew increasingly more feeble.

The tour headed to Augusta and the Masters. Ken, who had been hoping to remove that jinx, was virtually helpless there. Playing a practice round with Souchak, he learned that on holes where he had once hit a 5-iron approach, now he had to use a full 3-wood. Pain never left his hands now. They were permanently blanched and cold to the touch. The cortisone he had been taking in large amounts caused water retention and puffed out his body. He was forced to file off his ring because it was cutting into the flesh. He failed to survive the cut for the Masters. Finally, Souchak asked Venturi to call a physician friend of his at the Mayo Clinic in Rochester, Minnesota. Venturi left the tour immediately to see the doctor there.

Following extensive tests, the physician ordered Venturi off cortisone. This had to be done gradually to avoid withdrawal problems. The doctor told Venturi that he did not have Raynaud's Phenomenon. He believed Venturi had carpal tunnel syndrome, a strangulation of the median nerve, which controls feeling in the hand by a band of ligaments that encircles the palm side of the wrist much like subcutaneous handcuffs. That would account for the marked inability to grasp anything. Only surgery could verify or disprove the diagnosis. The physician advised an immediate operation, but Venturi deferred until he could defend his Open title in June. It was an obligation he would not break. He promised to return to the Mayo Clinic immediately afterward.

Venturi's slow reduction of cortisone did not prevent withdrawal problems. Without warning, he had periods of incredible rage when he smashed household furniture, times of deep depression and weeping, episodes of seeming amnesia during which he lost hours at a time and often found himself at their conclusion miles away from home.

Again he tried to play but with no more success than before. His hands were so weak that he began to paint his palms with a sticky resin so he wouldn't drop the golf club when he swung. He reached the Open, shot 81–79, and failed to make the cut for the final two rounds. He left for Rochester immediately. Surgery was scheduled for the following morning. (That evening, as Ken was undergoing tests, a man in a wheelchair came over to him. He told Venturi, "I am unable to use my arms or legs, but what has happened to you is one of the saddest things I've ever heard of. I just want you to know that you are always in my prayers because you have given so many people and so many of my friends the courage to keep going.")

The surgery consisted of cutting down to reach the band of ligament, then simply cutting it across and open to reduce pressure on the median nerve. Venturi, under a local anesthetic, listened as the band on the left hand was snipped (he likened the sound to the clipping of the metal binder around a crate of oranges) and heard the surgeon say, "Beautiful. Look at that nerve expand." The procedure was repeated with equal succss on the right hand. Venturi later was told that further delay could have meant the loss of the tips of the first two fingers on his right hand.

Venturi began a complex program of therapy to restore strength to his hands. His left hand responded quickly; his right posed a problem. His doctor told him he could expect difficulties in cold weather and that full recovery could not be predicted.

Ken rejoined the tour in early 1966 at the Lucky International, held at the course he had practiced on as a boy, Harding Park in San Francisco. It had been a year and a half since his last win, the American Golf Classic.

He shot 68–68–71 in the first three rounds to stay four strokes behind the leader, Frank Beard. He and Palmer were in fourth place. During one round, that was postponed because of freezing rain, and through the two last rounds Ken's father shuttled tubs of hot water to him from the kitchen so Ken could immerse his hands and keep them warm.

In the final round, Ken dropped birdie putts on six and nine to finish the front nine in 33. Beard and Palmer duplicated his score. Ken and Arnie now were tied for second place.

Venturi birdied 15 and 16 to take the lead. Beard bogied three holes. Palmer dropped back to par. Ken finished with a five-under-par 66 to defeat Beard by one stroke.

Although his hands still had not recovered, Ken had come back a second time to defeat a strong field.

It was fitting that the championship was where he had begun as a boy because his success didn't continue. As his game started to falter, he began to enter fewer tournaments. About 18 months later, Ken began to lose feeling again in his right hand. The symptoms recurred sporadically at first, then became steadily worse. He entered only seven tournaments in 1970 and placed in none. The right hand began to atrophy and in September 1970, immediate surgery was recommended.

This time, the operation was far more complicated. Scar tissue had formed over the nerves and tendons in the hand, preventing their full function. In a three-hour operation, surgeons had to scrape scar tissue from the nerves and tendons.

Now almost paranoid concerning his inability to win, Ken's first question to the surgeon when he woke was, "Was it my hand or my head?"

"It was your hand," the physician replied. "It was the worst-looking hand I've ever seen."

Ken never regained the strength he had in either hand. "When I lost my hands, I lost golf," he says now. "The kids on the tour today see me hit shots I never would have hit before and I know they're wondering, *How did he ever do what he did?*

Remarried and living in Palm Springs with his wife, Beau, with one son in college and the other in high school, Venturi now participates in fewer than a dozen tournaments a year. He spends much of his time telecasting golf and is, I think, one of the best golfer-commentators we have. His regrets are few. He had his full health for a bit less than eight of the 19 years since he turned pro in 1957; during that time, he won 16 tournaments and one major event, the '64 Open. One wonders how many he might have won if he had been well longer.

Wordsworth wrote, "Not in the clamour of the crowded streets, nor in the shouts and plaudits of the throng, but within ourselves are victory and defeat." Ken, I suspect, would agree with that. He may never play in the finals of the Masters or the Open again. But, for a brief period, before the strength was taken from his hands, Ken pushed aside his personal fears and uncounted medical ailments to stand again at the pinnacle of golf. Less than eight healthy years? What might he have accomplished? Ken probably doesn't trouble himself over that. He proved something very important to himself. And who else matters?

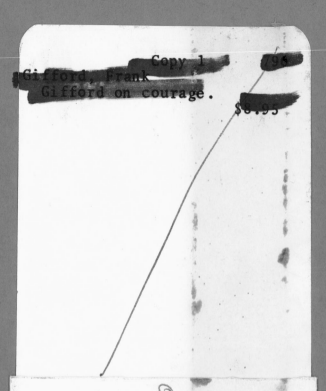

We would appreciate your returning this
Library item by the due date so that others
in the community may have use of this material.